Vocabulary Unplugged

30 Lessons That Will Revolutionize How You Teach Vocabulary K-12

Alana Morris

Discover Writing Press

Discover Writing Press

P.O. Box 264
Shoreham, Vermont 05770
1-800-613-8055
www.discoverwriting.com

Cover art by Robert Rehm
Book design by Bookwrights

ISBN# 1-931492-11-5

Library of Congress Control Number: 2004111630

   07 08 09   10 9 8 7 6 5 4 3

For information on seminars and more lesson plans call 1-800-613-8055
or visit our website at www.discoverwriting.com

For my brother, Randy,
who inspired me to keep digging,
and for my own "lexical vacuum cleaners,"
Corey and Kayce

Vocabulary Unplugged • ©2005 Alana Morris • www.discoverwriting.com

Table of Contents

Acknowledgments

I must deeply thank my children, Kayce and Corey, who have had to eat far more fast food during this adventure than any human should possibly consume. You both give me energy and hope, and within the entire *Oxford English Dictionary* there are not enough words to express how much I love you.

Prodigious thanks to the following:

My grandmothers, for providing lessons that never stop whispering. One was my literacy hero and the other a model of silent inner strength. I miss you both.

My mother, who has always been my dearest friend and who possesses wisdom that comes from some place deep and noble. I treasure what you have taught me.

John, who though we have our differences, has been there to lend great support; you are still my friend.

Dr. Joyce Carroll, who is an ongoing mentor and model, for her many lessons over the past 16 years.

Eddie Wilson, for having a true heart and an ingenious gift for creativity.

Gretchen Bernabei, for believing in my ideas and for always making me smile.

My friends and colleagues in Aldine who help make up our language arts seamless strand: Joyce Evans, Cherry Murrell, and Pam Byrne. We each have our special gifts and talents, which is why we are a team.

My dearest friends Bruce Goodner, Rhonda Clark, and Margaret Hale for never blocking my e-mails when they knew I was sending another chapter for review and suggestions. How can my neurons not be constantly massaged with friends like you?

My neurocentric sister, Karen Foster, who can see something positive in the most dismal moments.

My fellow Aldine NJWPT trainers: Tanisha Manning, Cindy Rogers, Linda Maxwell, Camille Hall, Pam Byrne, Jennifer Laughlin, Gwyn Manning, James Fons, Jesselyn Hall-Smith, Susan Perry, Candy Core, Amy Warren, Wendy Smith, Dorothy Ingram, Joyce Evans, Cindy Benge, Carrie Wilson, Michelle Becwar, and Arcelia Leon.

My fellow TCTELA board members and NHCCTE cohorts who help keep best practices and professionalism alive and well in Texas. There are no standards more important than solid teacher training and information: Mary Stockton, Linda Buie, Cathy Davis, Cindy Tyroff, Michael Guevara, Lynn Masterson, Cindy Benge, Sharon O'Neal, Dr. Linda Ellis, Cathy D'Entremont, Sharon Lewis, Michelle Becwar, Wilma Boone, Sally Rush, Jeannie Boyle, and Sylvia Rendon.

Dr. Wanda Bamberg, who lends her wisdom and support even when my passion's volume is REAL LOUD. Thanks for believing in me.

All of my colleagues in Aldine, for being the nation's best.

Introduction

Many of us, and certainly many of our students, would not have to undergo hypnosis to retrieve memories of dark classrooms, illuminated only by the dim light of an overhead projector, with the hypnotic fan humming a dusty lullaby in the background. The tedious assignment, in this cave-like setting, consisted of copying numerous vocabulary words, looking them up, and then using them in sentences. How many classroom hours were and still are utilized daily in this manner in the name of learning new words? How many lists are sent home each week with the assigned mission to seek mastery? It's my experience that the success rate for the words actually learned does not merit the time spent or the cost of the paper used to print the infamous lists. However, I also recognize that instruction year after year tends to repeat what came before—especially if it is not replaced by something offering greater prospects of success. So for decades the overhead/list model has continued to dominate the teaching of vocabulary.

At a young age, I knew I would become a teacher, not just because it was an incredibly noble profession, but because of my older brother, Randy.

Randy, was severely dyslexic, and his linguistic struggles haunted me even in childhood. How could someone so bright struggle in such incredible ways with words? He could take a broken television apart, and when he had miraculously reconstructed the hundreds of parts strewn all over the garage floor, the TV hummed with new life. I stood amazed because I knew I could never envision, much less complete, such a task. Yet when he was in the classroom and struggling to comprehend even basic text, the teachers could not see the intellect and brilliance that I so admired. The knowledge, research, and even protective laws regarding dyslexia, reading disorders, and struggling readers, in general, was in its infancy stage in the early 1970's. Rather than relying on his strengths and searching for other possible answers to decode text, he was made to feel inadequate, lazy, and unmotivated whenever he stepped into an academic setting. Traditional vocabulary study further increased his gap in literacy and assured him that printed words and language were not in his grasp—he was truly a child left behind. He dropped out of school mentally years before he was able to drop out physically. He later earned his G.E.D. and privately studied volumes of books on science, foreign language, and math, jotting thoughtful notes throughout the margins of the books he had purchased on his own or had been given as gifts. He loved learning; he simply didn't love school.

I knew there were answers somewhere out there to assist my brother with language, with words; and by becoming a teacher, I thought I would surely discover those mysterious answers. What I discovered, in addition to answers regarding students who struggle with words and language, is that there are far more students like my brother than I ever imagined, those who need more than a list of words and matching definitions.

I also saw myself in many of my students—those who had a good command of language, yet when required to memorize vocabulary and spelling words from isolated lists, could do remarkably well. I was adept at the memory game. Like me, these students could easily remember the words for quizzes and tests, but actually used few of the words afterward in their speech or writing. After the tests, the words were gone, lost somewhere in their neural pathways with slim hope of retrieval.

These scenarios paint a rather dismal picture of our lives as word users. If so many students have to struggle to learn word meanings, and others have such grave difficulties retrieving them, then it would seem that we must be a species with limited lexical prowess. Fortunately, this is not the case at all.

Steven Pinker (1994), cognitive psychologist and leading expert on language, says we begin using words around twelve months of age. "Therefore, high school graduates, who have been at it for about seventeen years, must have been learning an average of ten new words a day continuously since their first birthdays, or about a new word every ninety waking minutes" (Pinker 150). Likewise, he explains that preliterate children are "lexical vacuum cleaners," learning a new word every two waking hours. This means that our students are already plugged in—having learned numerous words before they ever set foot in our classrooms.

It also means that the estimated 13,000 words the average six-year-old commands were not learned from a list shown on an overhead projector, where the words were copied and then mindlessly used in sentences. Nor did these words emerge from lists given to all mothers, along with the diapers, formula, and coupons as mother and child were discharged and sent home from the hospital. These words were learned with seeming ease and obvious lexical brilliance, and what the thousands of words our students master and utilize without direct instruction have in common is that they were learned with a context and a purpose.

The purpose and goal of this book, then, is to share neurocentric ways to unplug vocabulary and spelling instruction so that words are not merely memorized in the name of the most current curriculum, but rather truly learned and owned by students. The goal is that the words actually permeate students' speech as well as their writing, thereby narrowing the gap between spoken and written discourse. The strategies shared are not bound to a specific age or grade level, because they draw on what we know about the brain, memory, and learning, whether the learner is five, fifteen, or seventy-nine. So slip inside these pages and unplug the distributed lists, unplug the passivity, unplug the overhead and dark classrooms, and discover the energy that emerges from the thirty activities and variations found when we plug in color, movement, poetry, history, music, and numerous other ways of exploring words within meaningful contexts.

Prologue
Plugging in Guidance

"Good planning, like good instruction, is as intentional as it is adaptable."
–David Pearson

Classroom Tempos

Time is movement. With careful consideration, we may even agree that without movement there would be no time. Photographers rely on time to catch moments—perfect moments that milliseconds later will be gone, altered by time. Musicians, too, rely on time for similar reasons. John Williams of the Boston Pops lifts his baton and smoothly sets the music in motion. Eighth notes collide against half notes in a dance that doesn't quite end even after the baton has circled around, signaling the end. Those few silent seconds directly after the instruments cease their vibrations are as tense and almost as critical as the downbeat that started the orchestra playing.

We, as teachers, have downbeats and cutoffs of our own, though we carry no baton to signal this reality. Our directions set things in motion, and the orchestrated balance between teaching and learning begins. Without even much rehearsal time, we can guide a well-constructed lesson that, like those final resonating sound waves in a good concert hall, will leave our students with lingering thoughts about the concepts and ideas we deliver. But one missed beat, one detail out of tune, one missing player—and our cognitive concerto gets hideous reviews from our most important critics: our students.

Lessons cannot be planned haphazardly and without giving thought to pacing, learning styles, attention levels, and the myriad of other brain-appropriate considerations that must be taken into account for the diverse learners we work with each day. Teaching is not simply a professional delivery system where content is merely "covered." Instead, teaching is the fine art of creating, facilitating, getting out of the way, stepping in at the right time, readjusting at critical moments, fine-tuning the rough spots, and then celebrating achievements. Timing is essential in everything we do in the classroom.

The Gradual Release Model

If you study any recent book on reading instruction, you will more than likely come across Pearson and Gallagher's Gradual Release Model (see diagram on page ix). Concepts and/or skills are taught to students in well-planned lessons that begin with teachers directly teaching, modeling, and then gradually moving students toward independence. Throughout the lesson, the teacher provides feedback and guidance and assures real-text application of concepts and strategies. This model, though seemingly simple, requires the same practice, precision, and patience needed by the symphony conductor.

The Gradual Release Model actually works well in a variety of contexts. Last year, for example, my son expressed a strong, almost overwhelming fear of drowning. Though he had taken swimming lessons numerous times in the past, he still felt insecure about his safety in the water and his ability to effectively swim. I finally had to concede that I had wasted my money on previous attempts to build his competency as a swimmer. So I decided to sign him up for private lessons with a swim instructor at the health club where I work out. Within two lessons, not only was he swimming, but he also *believed he was a swimmer*. He felt safe in the water. He continued for several more lessons, while I, who always enjoy observing master teachers, marveled at the instructor's natural ability to guide his success. How had she done it?

Each lesson began with the instructor observing my son as he applied the strokes and skills she had taught him the week before, followed by kind reminders and comments such as, "Watch again, your arm must stay closer to your body like this," and she would model precisely the desired position of his head, arms, and body. He then immediately gave it a shot. Her praise and encouragement gave him confidence as he advanced to more difficult strokes and accomplishments. She stayed right beside him in the water for much of the lesson as she watched, readjusted, and moved him along from one skill to the next. She immediately corrected any bad habits or patterns forming by remodeling and redirecting once again. Before the lesson ended each week, she would make a point of getting my attention (as if I were not already completely tuned in) to allow him to show me how well he was swimming.

Vocabulary instruction requires the same careful planning, modeling, guidance, and application of newly explored words. Simply defining words and using them in sentences is like my son taking lessons each summer without truly learning to swim. He received instruction, he moved around in the water, and he progressed through a series of badges that showed his process: tadpole, turtle, fish, and even the infamous shark. But the reality was that he was not confident as a swimmer, and even after numerous lessons, he still feared drowning. He needed instruction, modeling, and guided practice before being released to practice and master swimming skills on his own. In the same way, we must instruct, model, do guided practice, and then gradually release students from simply "knowing" words to actually owning and using them in real contexts.

Lessons in *Vocabulary Unplugged*

As part of my position in the district where I serve as language arts program director for grades 5–8, I work closely with teachers of reading and writing. Even among master teachers and in some of my own lessons, I've found that guided practice often receives less attention. In some classrooms, even with well-intentioned teachers, the lessons progress straight from discussion to independent practice. Assessment for mastery soon follows, and teachers often beat themselves up when they see the poor results. After all their hard work, students have still not mastered the skills and concepts taught, making it seem as if little or no instruction had actually occurred.

The last fifteen years of brain research has provided numerous clues as to how the brain learns and processes information. Each day new studies shed further light on the mysteries of learning and retaining the information we have learned. Each chapter in this book challenges you to plug in an area of research that enhances learning, such as memory, color, music, patterns, context, history, and so forth. Following brief information about these important areas, lessons are presented that, in most cases, employ Pearson and Gallagher's Gradual Release Model. The lessons are not intended to be scripts of any kind, but rather guidelines. In these guidelines, however, crucial points of the lesson are present that will help ensure success for all learners.

Have fun exploring words with your students; change the lessons as needed to fit your kids, your personality, and your strengths as a teacher. *Unplug* what isn't working and *plug in* the energy from lessons that build a community of learners who aren't afraid of the water and are willing to dive into the deep end... and swim.

Gradual Release Model
Pearson and Gallagher

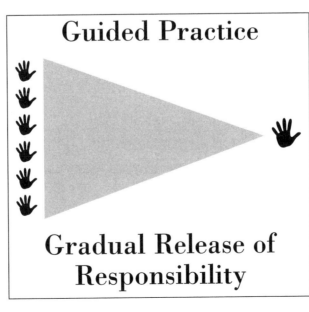

Teacher	Collaboration (with peers and teacher)	Student
Modeling and Instruction (occurs throughout the lesson, not just at the beginning)	**Guided Practice** / **Gradual Release of Responsibility**	**Independent Practice and Authentic Application**

Chapter 1
Plugging In Memory

"Memorizing keeps us in the past; forgetting forces us into the present."

—Ellen Langer

Students Are Not Computers

Modern life without computers would certainly cause great stress. I do not know how I made it to the sixth grade before our family purchased our first Commodore 64 computer. Even with this slower, early model, I was amazed that I could input information and return days, even weeks later to find my information, undisturbed where I had stored it.

Technology has advanced tremendously over the past couple of decades and will continue to progress. We have memory sticks for our cameras and portable memory sticks for storing and transferring vast amounts of data. We often make analogies between computer devices and our own brains. Even though educators should know better, we often assume that we *download files* into rows of eager and motivated *hard drives* who will be able to retrieve that information when called upon to do so.

However, a huge fallacy exists. The human mind truly does not function like a computer system. The human mind loses important details, fails to file information that others may deem vital, and miscodes data, causing it to reappear when least expected—or not at all. The bottom line is that we, as educators, cannot download files into eagerly waiting hard drives and assume that it can be retrieved when needed. What we must do is learn as much as possible about how the human brain processes, stores, and retrieves information.

Who has not experienced the frustration of being unable to locate keys or glasses, or trying to recall someone's name at a party without success, or struggling to remember details of a conversation that took place weeks ago? And what is it that's gone wrong in a complex system that would allow a famous musician to leave his $2.5 million cello in the trunk of a New York taxi?

These memory errors are not signs of a diseased brain; they are the realities of the normal human mind: a curse and a blessing, a series of checks and balances that allow us to function at high levels day in and day out. We tend to focus on the negative aspects of memory, but the abilities of this system are truly amazing, and in most cases it serves us remarkably well.

The Human Memory System

The human memory system is the ultimate multitasker (sorry, Windows XP). Many memory tasks are utilized and, more important, *required* for language acquisition, including vocabulary—for comprehension, for decoding texts, and so forth. In efforts to better understand the complexities of working with words, educators would advance their pedagogical practices by, above all else, understanding the complexities of the human memory system(s)—how it works, the brain areas involved, how it may be improved, and how common memory errors might impact the act of reading and learning words.

Theories and observations of human memory go back at least to Aristotle, with his examination of the laws of association. For years the quest for the seat of memory consumed much of the work of neurological studies. However, there is no one single location where memory is found. Research has indicated that memory "is not a single organ like the heart or liver, but an alliance of systems that work together, allowing us to learn from the past and predict the future" (Baddeley [1999] 1).

One of the first early scientific explorers of memory, who provided systematic evidence for his discoveries, was Hermann Ebbinghaus, German psychologist, in 1885. He gave us the first glimpse of *transience*, the most common memory issue we all experience. He explored the rate at which the information fades from memory, which is what neurologists and psychologists call transience. His early discovery that information fades most rapidly directly after the learning has been confirmed in numerous studies. Due to transience and other problems with our complex memory system, we must employ a variety of strategies for exploring vocabulary.

Research on memory has continued to advance at a steady and at times even explosive pace. Today the use of MRI's and PET scans has brought advanced technology into the picture and has allowed researchers to examine memory not only from a psychological perspective but also from a cognitive, physiological view.

The following are only a sampling of memory theories that have developed throughout the years of research:

- Locale/Taxon memory
- Short Term/Long Term Memory (late 1950s)
- Working Memory: Central Executive, Phonological Loop, Visio-Spatial Sketchpad (Alan Baddeley)
- Episodic, Procedural, Semantic Memory Systems

For every question answered in the field of memory, there are just as many questions added to the inquiry. Daniel Schacter, a leading expert on memory, has examined the errors of memory in a systematic fashion. In his book *Seven Sins of Memory: How the Mind Forgets and Remembers*, he illustrates seven memory problems that we encounter most frequently. Rather than "sins," in classroom discussions I like to call these memory difficulties "memory warps."

Naturally, many of these memory issues are observed in the process of reading and vocabulary study. Much of what affects our day-to-day lives regarding memory also impacts our ability to learn, remember, and retrieve words.

The seven memory sins outlined by Schacter are transience, absentmindedness, blocking, misattribution, suggestibility, bias, and perseverance. Each impacts reading in one way or another, but three are crucial to successfully remembering words we have learned through various contexts. Transience, absentmindedness, and blocking are the three memory problems that have the greatest impact on how we remember words.

Transience

The first problem, *transience*, is the most common and involves the weakening or loss of memory over time. In this sense, the brain functions like my wardrobe. When cleaning out my closet, I set aside or get rid of those articles of clothing that I no longer need or wear. If I have not worn it in over a year, chances are I am not going to wear it in the future. So it is discarded. Much the same process happens with memories in our brains. The connections keeping a specific memory accessible begin to dissipate when that information is deemed no longer necessary by the brain. Mental chaos would ensue if we held on to every bit of information ever processed in our brains. Imagine keeping every article of clothing you have ever owned—whether it is fashionable any longer or not, whether it fits anymore or not! It would not be a workable system, to say the least.

The same is true of the brain and its wardrobe of memories, its walk-in closet of information. Research studies have also shown that transience is influenced by what happens as people register or encode the information being processed. More elaboration (focus and attention on details) during encoding produces less transient memories. Encoding is the process of creating a solid memory trace; it is the birth of a memory. "The better the quality of this memory trace, the greater the probability that a stable long-term memory representation will result" (Baddeley [1993] 71). This is a crucial idea for learning new words. If students are not properly encoding the words, they are wasting time and energy because the words will fade before transferring over to long-term memory where they can later be retrieved.

Absentmindedness

Absentmindedness is the second memory problem Schacter brings to light. This is a memory error that occurs when the information was never encoded properly or is available but overlooked when we need it. Absentmindedness illustrates the importance of attention in the encoding process. He explains, "One way to prevent elaborative encoding is to disrupt or divide attention when people are acquiring new information" (Schacter [2001] 44). Tim Shallice in neuroimaging studies highlighted in Schacter's book has illustrated that "dividing attention prevents the left frontal lobe from playing its normal role in elaborative encoding" (45).

Automatic or routine behaviors in our day-to-day lives are a main source of absentminded memory errors. For example, my drive home from work is routine and automatic. I travel the same route every day without deviation. One day last week I needed to stop on the way home to pick up my daughter's prescription, and I reminded myself several times throughout the day. However, once I began the trek home, at the same time of day, down the same road, with the same traffic, the routine took over. It was not until I got ready to give my daughter her medicine later that evening that I remembered the task that was left unaccomplished.

Absentmindedness may be associated with low levels of activity in the left pre-frontal lobe. As with transience, the left prefrontal area of the brain is highly activated in imaging studies where the participant is elaborating on incoming information. Automatic behaviors require no new incoming information and therefore leave the memory system vulnerable to errors.

Two types of memory are influenced by absentmindedness: retrospective memory and prospective memory. *Retrospective* memory deals with memories of past events and details, as well as facts learned in the past (your high school graduation day, the state capitals), whereas *prospective* memory involves remembering to do things in the future (turning out a light, keeping an appointment, making a phone call). Schacter points out an interesting social issue related to these two memory types. When someone has a retrospective memory failure, society tends to see *memory as unreliable*. If someone's prospective memory fails, *the person is seen as unreliable*. However, both types of memory operate within the same complex memory system.

Prospective memory is divided into event-based and time-based memory tasks. Event-based tasks require carrying out a particular task based on an event ("When you see Pam, tell her to call her doctor"). *Time-based* tasks require carrying out an action at a particular time (taking medicine, turning a document in, paying a bill.) Memory cues should be available when the action needs performing. The old idea of tying a string around the finger falls short in that it is not specific enough. Neville's Remembrall in *Harry Potter and the Sorcerer's Stone* fails for the same reason. When the glowing red reminder arrives, poor Neville has no idea what he has forgotten.

Studying New Words

Where the research on automatic encoding comes into play for reading is in the areas of vocabulary and focused studying. The conclusion drawn here is not new, but the imaging explorations are. Through neuroimaging studies, it has been illustrated that spaced study and studying frequently are preferred to cramming. What literally happens at a chemical and cellular level is that when the brain becomes familiar with incoming information, it pays less attention to that information. Therefore attention levels drop. Repeating the information at close intervals causes automatic encoding because the brain is already familiar with the information. Automatic encoding is associated with reduced left prefrontal activity and poorer subsequent memory. When the information is delivered at more widely spaced intervals, it is less familiar each time and the left prefrontal lobe is activated for better learning.

Blocking

One of the most irritating memory problems is *blocking*—the inability to retrieve information when you need it. This dilemma is frustrating because it feels as if the word you want to use is within mental reach, but you cannot retrieve it at the time. Names are the most often blocked bits of information. When we are trying to recall proper names, the region in the front of the left temporal lobe known as the temporal pole is activated. "The memory system is being asked to make the fragile link between a person's characteristics and the arbitrary label by which he or she is known to others" (Schacter [2001] 71).

In 1966, Harvard psychologists Roger Brown and David McNeill brought the first investigation of what we now know as Tip-of-the-Tongue (TOT) state. Schacter explains the feeling of this state as "the unmistakable sensation of being on the brink of a sneeze" (75).

Many other languages have expressions using "the tongue" to explain blocking:

Italian	*sulla punta della lingue*
Afrikaans	*op die punt van my tong*
Estonian	*keele otsa peal* (or at the head of the tongue)
Cheyenne	*navonotootse`a* (I have lost it on my tongue)
Korean	*kyeu kkedu-te mam-dol-da* (sparkling at the tip of my tongue)

Often words come to mind that are not the sought-after word. James Reason, a British psychologist, labeled these intrusive words "ugly sisters." "Through their close relation to the target, ugly sisters may attract undue attention and interfere with retrieval of the sought-after item" (Schacter [2001] 75). For example, while trying recently to recall one of my saxophone professors from the University of North Texas, I kept thinking, "Richter." I knew the name started with an "R." I also knew her first name was Debbie. Her last name was actually Richtmeyer. The more I thought about "Richter," the longer I was unable to retrieve "Richtmeyer." "Richter" was the "ugly sister" in this case.

Further investigation suggests that while ugly sisters do not necessarily cause blocking, they may prolong the TOT state. To assist in relieving blocking, utilizing the alphabet is helpful because the first letter of the blocked word is generally known. Likewise, avoid repeating or focusing on ugly sisters. Students often hang onto the gist of learned words but cannot retrieve the exact word he or she seeks. Understanding what we know about blocking will be helpful for all learners.

Opening Up the Package

Our new understandings of memory are shedding light on the successes, the struggles, and the possibilities in retaining information. Dr. Joyce Carroll states, "We learn and remember what has meaning; we have difficulty remembering and easily forget what does not" (24). We can apply what we know about memory to bring meaning to the study of words. For lasting memory to occur, the brain has to be taken beyond the obvious. Unfortunately, this sometimes fails to happen within classrooms and in learning episodes at all levels. Ellen Langer (1997) discusses the dangers of this linear, fact-based learning: "If we simply memorize the known past, we are not preparing ourselves for the as-yet-to-be-known future" (81). This is not a dilemma peculiar to public education systems; it is a dilemma based on old paradigms about learning that were not grounded in biological realities or discoveries about the processes of memory. "Closed packages of information are taken as facts. Facts are to be taken as absolute truths to be learned as is, to be memorized, leaving little reason to think about them. Without any reason to open the package, there is little chance that the information will lead to any conceptual insights or even be rethought in a new context" (Langer 71).

We must offer and allow learners to open these packages of knowledge, not simply force them to memorize the wrapping. The gift they will find waiting inside is the ability to retrieve information more readily, to search for and find patterns that will lead to greater understanding of concepts, and to build dynamic neural pathways through the process.

The strategies explored in this chapter and the entire book will utilize what we know about our complex memory system in order to minimize transience, absentmindedness (divided attention) and blocking by enhancing vocabulary instruction at the encoding and rehearsal levels.

Word Storm

Rationale:

Vocabulary words are not fully learned until students actually use them in their written and/or spoken language. Simply memorizing lists of words for the sake of weekly assessments or to aid in reading a story does not ensure the acquisition of the words in the long term. The residue of words that lingers days, weeks, months, and years later is evidence of learning and solid language instruction.

Word Storm allows students to periodically "vacuum" up the residue of words they have stored. These words have settled into their long-term memory and may or may not ever be utilized in their writing or speech. Again, storage is not the problem; *retrieval* is. When students are guided to rehearse words at spaced intervals, transience is lessened and both teachers and students can examine patterns of strengths and areas of concern around knowledge of various word patterns and structures.

Objectives:

The students will, within a set time period, write down as many words as possible (from one syllable to six syllables) in order to retrieve words they have been exposed to, words they are familiar with, and words they know and use regularly.

Materials:

Word Storm transparency and/or poster board for modeling

Presentation Guidelines:

- As with any lesson, modeling is important for Word Storm. Use a transparency or poster board to walk students through the thinking process and procedures for experiencing a Word Storm.
- Have students briefly discuss what they know about storms in the atmosphere. Possible comments:
  –Conditions have to be right
  –Sometimes fast
  –Sometimes slow
  –Rain or snow does not fall all at once
  –Can indicate danger
  –Can be beneficial
- Explain that the Word Storm is a mental storm that will have many of the same characteristics of a typical weather storm and that the purpose is to write down whatever comes to mind.

- Initially, as the students are learning the process for the first time, do not put any stipulations on the types of words they can include for the storm. Accept any and all words this first time around.

- Model the process on the transparency or poster board by adding the first couple of words. Model higher-level words and the types of words you want the students to use (for the developmental level with which you work). If words such as *the* and *go* are modeled, these are the types of words the students will give as well.

- After a few words have been modeled, allow students to provide words. Make a **BIG DEAL** out of words they provide that are higher level. Accept all answers. A student may provide a word that he or she believes has three syllables, whereas it actually has four syllables. This is a great time to utilize the **Syllable Squat** (chapter four) to bring movement to the process of exploring syllables.

- Once you and the students feel confident that they understand this process, then move the students toward independence.

- Allow students to complete their first Word Storm with a partner or in a group. Again, this is critical for scaffolding learning. If we release students to independence too rapidly, we will be disappointed with the results. This is true in any of the lessons throughout the book and with learning in general, as discussed with the Gradual Release Model in chapter one.

- Finally, students will be ready to independently experience a Word Storm. At this point, specific Word Storms can be employed.

•math words•geography words•adjectives, verbs, etc.•long I words and/or other patterns•science words•

The following example comes from fifth-grade student, Ruth Hernandez; Stehlik Intermediate School—Houston, Texas. The class was asked to brainstorm science words.

WORD STORM

1 Syllable	2 Syllables	3 Syllables	4 Syllables	5 Syllables	6 Syllables
Acid	machines	elements	insulators	evaporation	Periodic table
Base	space	scientist	velocity	accelerator	Paleontologist
labs	matter	gravity	experiments		
mass	Matter	chemical	Viscosity		
		motion			

- After the Word Storm, have students draw a line under the words they have added as pictured in the previous example.
- A good practice, at this point, is to allow students to find five to ten additional words by using a dictionary, a thesaurus, or another source.

Evaluation/Variations:

- Grading is easy for the Word Storm. However, you may choose to alter the point system as the year progresses or based on developmental needs. For example, you may later decide to give half a point for one-syllable words rather than a full point.

1 syllable=1 point

2 syllables=2 points

3 syllables=3 points

4 syllables=4 points

5 syllables=5 points

6 syllables=6 points

- Encourage students to include words in each column and to randomly skip between the columns as they are adding words. The brain naturally will jump from one word to another and the words will not necessarily be of the same syllable count. It would be incredibly unnatural to ask students to progress from one column to the next.
- Each subsequent Word Storm should yield more words and more advanced words. This is one of the best ways to assess progress.
- Encourage students to reflect on how they did on the Word Storm and set goals for subsequent storms.
- Ask students to categorize the words from the Word Storm (nouns, verbs, adjectives, homonyms, etc.).
- Ask students to circle the three most unique words on their list.
- Add all new six-syllable words, written on large index cards or sentence strips, to a special publishing location in the room. (The ceiling tiles are an awesome place!)
- Make sure, where possible, that students know the definitions of the words on their Word Storms. Any and all words generated can be used with the strategies suggested throughout the book to ensure high-level understanding of the words.
- Some teachers who work with younger students may be tempted to only have up to three syllables on the Word Storm chart. Though many younger students may not be able to generate numerous multisyllabic words, it is a grand challenge, and the brain LOVES challenges. Change the scoring scale rather than the chart. This way, all students win!

WORD STORM

1 Syllable	2 Syllables	3 Syllables	4 Syllables	5 Syllables	6 Syllables

Word Connections

Rationale:

Understanding that the brain constantly and naturally seeks connections will greatly benefit word study. Students need to make numerous connections with words in order to truly comprehend the meaning(s) of acquired words. Memory and high-level comprehension are enhanced through the metacognitive process of making connections.

Likewise, the more neural areas within the brain where a word is stored (color, movement, music, and so forth), the greater the possibility for retrieval. The potential for blocking is lessened when the words are being stored in multiple locations within the brain's neural pathways and when the words are used frequently.

Objectives:

Students will explore words by making connections with weather conditions, colors, seasons, and music. They must be able to justify their answers. They can make these connections only when they understand the words at a deep conceptual level.

Materials:

Transparency of Word Connections grid or poster board
Markers, crayons, or colored pencils

Presentation Guidelines:

- Set up the lesson by discussing the importance of connecting new information to previously learned concepts. Adhesive Velcro works well to illustrate this idea. Have students place one side of the Velcro on the left pointer finger and the corresponding piece of Velcro on the right pointer finger. The left side represents previously learned concepts; the right side represents new information that is to be learned. Show how when the two fingers come together, the new information connects with the old information and sticks. This is how the process of learning occurs in the brain.
- Model the process of Word Connections with a transparency or a poster board.
- Example: If the word is *crescendo*, ask students what weather condition *crescendo* is most like.
- Possible suggestion: "*Crescendo* is like a tornado."
- The student should then be asked why *crescendo* is like a tornado. The answer is meaningless without the justification.
- Possible response: "A crescendo is like a tornado because it starts out small and then builds to a stronger, more forceful level."

- Model using an illustration to make the connection visible. The illustration does not have to be incredibly artistic. Using the idea of a desktop icon may help students who do not feel confident about their drawing abilities. The illustration can be anything from a stick figure to a magazine-clipped image.

- At the close of the modeling of this strategy, each box will include the appropriate connection (What weather condition, color, season, and song is crescendo most like?), an illustration for each connection, and the explanation, clearly written, of how the word connects to the concept in each box.

- The characteristics of the words should be completed last. This step gives the students an opportunity to truly analyze the word at a high level. Now that they understand the word at a high level, what is known about the word?

    •part of speech•sound patterns•syllables•country of origin•what areas might it be used•

    Word: **crescendo**   Characteristic(s) of word: noun, 3 syllables, musical term, comes from Italian and Latin

- Students should now be guided through a Word Connection chart either with a partner or in a group before moving to full independence. This will help to clarify any misconceptions about the process of making connections in this way. By modeling effectively and guiding the instruction, you will be helping your students learn words at higher levels.

Evaluation/Variations:

- A rubric or point system works well to measure mastery on the Word Connection activity.

    24 points per quadrant: Answer = 5 points

    Illustration = 4 points

    Justification = 15 points

    4 points for the word characteristics

- Vary the concepts within the quadrants if you would like (certainly not necessary since the words will change). Any of the four concepts within the quadrants might be changed to emotion, flower, book, etc.

- The benefits of this strategy come from the multilayered examination of the word and the fact that students must know the word at the conceptual level to complete the tasks.

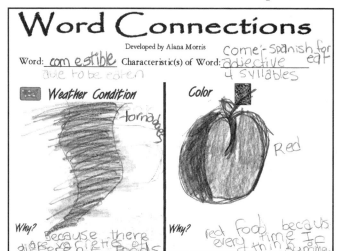

Corey Morris,
6th grade example
for the word comestible

Word Connections

Developed by Alana Morris

Word: _____   Characteristic(s) of Word:

Weather Condition

Why?

Color

Why?

Season

Why?

Song

Why?

Word Walls

Rationale:

Like many learning ideas that have become commercialized, Word Walls have become a buzzword—a prepackaged, waiting-to-be-laminated teacher tool that can be found at most teacher stores. They are often purchased and placed on walls by teachers who are required to have Word Walls. And there they stay. But just "having" word walls is not effective. *Have* is a linking verb and/or a helping verb. What we need is full-blown ACTION. Our students must *use* the Word Walls we have.

Research on episodic memory (see Plugging in Memory) has gained much strength in the past decade. Students at many law schools are now allowed to study in the rooms where their bar exams will be taken due to solid evidence that learners score better on exams taken in the room where the material is learned or rehearsed. This is because the environment of the rooms serves as a memory hook for the information being learned. Likewise, students score better on tests when the teacher is present versus absent. The teacher is actually an "episode" that triggers recall of important information for students. Knowing the strength of the environment for memory formations drives the purpose for using a variety of Word Walls that serve multiple objectives.

Word Walls to assist young readers and writers are not new. Though sometimes the words remain static on the walls, gathering dust, many teachers use them effectively as a learning and teaching tool that enhances reading and writing instruction in the classroom.

By expanding our idea of Word Walls to Pattern Walls, where students are encouraged to explore patterns among words, we enhance the possibilities for exposure to, experience with, and exploration of words for dynamic, varied purposes. Our walls should drip with words that explode with ongoing meaning for our students—figuratively speaking, of course!

The following lesson will illustrate one Word Wall that focuses on word play (chapter three). The lesson is followed by a list of one hundred possible Word Walls. Actually, there are thousands of possibilities for such Word Walls. Only the students and the curriculum can determine what Word Wall may be most beneficial at any given time. Throughout *Vocabulary Unplugged*, lessons will generate possible Word Walls that are authentic and scream to the students, "Look at me! Think about me!" And because the students have ownership in the process, they can figuratively scream back, "Thank you. I will."

Objective(s):

Students will participate in the creation, rotation, and exploration of a Word Wall that examines "ricochet words" (zigzag, flip-flop, nitwit, etc.). Words will be added as they are discovered.

Materials:

Poem: "Ode to my Southern Drawl" by Kathi Appelt from *Poetry After Lunch*
      (or any poem or selection dealing with the way words sound)
Book: *Double Trouble in Walla Walla* by Andrew Clements
Sentence strips or large index cards
Markers
Walls

Presentation Guideline:

- Discuss with students how authors, songwriters, and advertisers often choose words based on how they sound. Have them brainstorm words they like based on how they sound. A personal favorite is *drizzle*. I like the way it sounds and how it appears to disappear inside the mouth. Provide one of your favorites and then generate a list of the students' favorites.

- Read Kathi Appelt's "Ode to My Southern Drawl" (or any poem or selection dealing with the way words sound).

- Share with students that there is a special subset of words called "ricochet words." The words bounce off each other and create a unique rhythm to the ear. They're paired words that differ either only in a vowel (*tick-tock, mish-mash*) or a consonant (*hoity-toity, lovey-dovey*). The official name that linguists give ricochet words is *reduplicative compounds*.

     •willy-nilly•zigzag•hanky-panky•pitter-patter•flip-flop•nitty-gritty•tip-top•crisscross•

- See if students can come up with additional ricochet words.

- Read *Double Trouble in Walla Walla* by Andrew Clements. Have students generate a Personal Word Wall (see handout on page 17) as they listen to the story. Ask them to add the ricochet words they hear in pencil, as they may want to change the spellings later. Ricochet words can be tricky to spell.

- After the story, ask students to share the ricochet words they heard. Discuss what characteristics the words share and where and how authors, songwriters, and/or advertisers would use these types of words.

- Ask students to brainstorm, with a partner, places (songs, commercials, movies, books, traditional sayings, etc.) where they have heard these words. Share as a class.

- Each student should adopt one of the ricochet words to add to the class Word Wall. If you have multiple classes, each student should only create one so that students throughout the day will be able to add a word to the Word Wall. Illustrations are a great way to add color to the Ricochet Word Wall.

- Students should add a card below their ricochet word, defining its meaning.

- Throughout the next week, students should be on the lookout for more ricochet words from their reading and other locations. Add these words to the wall as they are brought in.

Evaluation/Variations:

Multiple steps of this activity can be assessed if desired. However, not all assignments need a grade. What is most crucial is feedback. The following works well for breaking down possible points. Using a rubric is the best way to assess performance-based tasks that require color, illustrations, multiple steps, writing, etc.

-Personal Word Wall of words from Double Trouble in Walla Walla (20 points)

-Ricochet word created for the Word Wall (40 points)

-Definition of the ricochet word's meaning (40 points)

100 Word Wall Possibilities

Government Words	Verbs	Animal Words	Big Words	Names	Music Words	Cold Words	Clothing Words	Synonyms	Science Words
Compound Words	Bird Words	Long "A" Words	Ricochet Words	Story Words	Writing Words	Long "I" Words	Electric Words	Math Words	Danger Words
Traditional Alphabetized Word Walls	Walking Words	Words about dishes	Words Borrowed from other Countries	Funny Words	Vehicle Words	Double Consonant Words	Reading Words	Emotion Words	World War II Words
Time Words	Number Words	Poetry Words	School Words	Nouns	Unique Words	Insect Words	Danger Words	Money Words	Memory Words
Homophones	Long "E" Words	Loud Words	Water Words	Foot Words	Weather Words	Long "O" Words	Manners Words	Energy Words	Rodeo Words
Technology	Beach Words	Food Words	Adverbs	Family Words	High Frequency Words	Newspaper Words	Election Words	Pizza Words	Pioneer Words
Oxymoron	Words about Words	Glamorous Words	Earth Words	Love Words	Hot Words	Dancing Words	Old Words	Feeling Words	Motion Words
Animation Words	Rhyming Words	Scary Words	Words with Prefixes	Cooking Words	Latin Words	Words with Suffixes	Three syllable Words	Trouble Words	Double Vowel Words
Commonly Misspelled Words	Garden Words	Recycling Words	Words for "said"	Words ending in –ee	Social Words	Colonial Words	Pain Words	Six Syllable Words	Zoo Words
Geography	Sweet Words	Spanish Words	Mysterious Words	Party Words	Geometry Words	Slang Words	Weird Words	Sky Words	Sports Words

Personal, Portable Word Wall

Chapter 2
Plugging In Wordplay

Wordplay: No Bling Bling Required

"What's in a name? that which we call a rose/ By any other name would smell as sweet…" (2.2.45-46)

What Shakespeare knew well and verbally illustrated in the famous line from *Romeo and Juliet* was that there is much in a name and much to every word. Words give power, cause pain, win and lose elections, and provide us with hours of fun—and play. *Wordplay* is literally a game of intelligence. Jokes, riddles, puns, and humor in general are all forms of wordplay and ways in which we mentally manipulate language.

Puns such as "Make like a tree and leaf" only have an impact on someone who has the ability to mentally transpose *leaf* to *leave* and find humor in the sound play used. A good pun will elicit one of two common reactions—a grin or a groan. Either should be considered a sign of success in the game of wordplay.

The English language has always lent itself to wordplay. Evidence of the love of linguistic play can be found as far back as the earliest speakers of what would become English, the Anglo-Saxons. The beginnings of our language and our playfulness with language were oral. Epic poems such as *Beowulf* were spoken out loud by bards and entertained listeners for hours. Back then—before MTV, DVDs, CDs, MP3s, radios, jukeboxes, or movies—it was the sounds and patterns of the words themselves that breathed rhythm into the stories and carried powerful meanings to their audiences.

The Elizabethan Age and William Shakespeare provide later, written examples of our love of wordplay. Shakespeare was truly a great wordsmith, coining hundreds of words that are still in use today, such as *eyeball, gloomy,* and *unaware*. His extraordinary use of wordplay, especially puns, brought wit and cleverness to the stories in his plays, whether the plot was humorous, historical, or tragic in nature. Notice the use of wordplay in this brief excerpt from *Hamlet*. Rosencrantz and Guildenstern are trying to get Hamlet to talk to them about what's bothering him—about the "cause" of his "distemper," in Rosencrantz's phrase. Some musicians come upon the scene and Hamlet suggests that Guildenstern pick up one of the instruments (a pipe) and play it. Guildenstern says he cannot; he doesn't know how. This is Hamlet's response:

> …and there is much music, excellent voice, in this little organ; yet cannot you make it speak. 'Sblood, do you think I am easier to be played on than a pipe? Call me what instrument you will, though you can fret me, yet you cannot play upon me.
> *Hamlet* III, ii, 360–65

Audiences continue to marvel at Shakespeare's wit and playfulness with the English language. Yet just over two thousand years ago, there was no English language. Today, after centuries of invasions, battles, migrations, and merchant travel throughout the world, the English language is alive, well, and spoken by more people than any other language. English also contains more words (over a billion) than any other language. No wonder it is often so hard to find just the right word. There are so many choices!

The English language is a mixture of Old English (Anglo-Saxons), Latin (from the Roman priests who brought Christianity to England), Old Norse (from the Vikings), Norman-French (from the Normans), and thousands of borrowed words from all over the world. Such a diverse bank of words, full of synonyms and homonyms, allows our language to be incredibly precise and provides almost limitless opportunity for sound and wordplay. The more one knows about the language and the words of the language, the better the game!

Words Borrowed (never returned) from Other Countries

Italy	Spain	Iran	Arabia	India
piano	tornado	chess	syrup	shampoo
carnival	vanilla	paradise	coffee	bandana
violin	mosquito	bazaar	zero	pajamas

Unlike Latin, which in considered a dead language, English is alive and kicking. It is considered a living language that, like the people who speak it, continues to change and grow. The new edition of the *Oxford English Dictionary* (OED), released in June of 2003, now has roughly 400,000 words and phrases. This is only the third time in 146 years that the dictionary has been revised. Can you imagine the amount of new words that had to be added? The answer is over 6,000! Where in the world do new words come from? The table below will shed light on where some of the new words and phrases appearing in the new version of the OED came from. Many, if not all, of these words were created during your lifetime.

Entertainment/media	Medical Field	Literature/print	Technology
Yadda yadda yadda	primary care	Muggles (*Harry Potter*)	search engines
bling bling	botox	Orcs (*Lord of the Rings*)	multitask
FX (as in special effects)	caregiver	webzines	chatroom
Pay-per-view	nutraceutical		double-click

These additions further enhance the usefulness and playfulness of our language. The list of wordplay possibilities is almost endless. Puns, limericks, riddles, anagrams, palindromes, Scrabble, Boggle, crossword puzzles, jokes, cryptograms—all offer wordsmiths hours of cheaper-than-cable fun.

One example of wordplay is called Anguish Languish, created by Howard Chance. In Anguish Languish, the creator replaces an actual text with words that sound remarkably close to the original. For example, *hello* may become *halo*. See if you can decode this set of imposters to determine what Anguish Languish nursery rhyme is given below.

> Marry hatter ladle limb
> Itch fleas worse widest snore.
> An ever-wear debt Marry win
> Door limb was shorter gore.

So, why do people love the idea of Peter Piper picking pickled peppers, or a fellow named Sam who eats green eggs and ham? How do stand-up comedians like Chris Rock and Robin Williams bring an audience to uncontrolled laughter in fewer than fifty words? The answer lies in the words themselves. In their sounds, in their homophones and double meanings, in their ability to change like a chameleon depending on the context, and in their complexity, we find room to play. The grandest aspect of wordplay is that it is accessible to everyone who speaks English. We own our words. We own our language. So put aside your bling bling and don't be a Muggle. Go ahead and play; it's free.

By Alana Morris © 2003 by Region IV Education Service Center. Reprinted with permission.

Galumphing: The Power of Play in Learning

When the idea of *play* comes to mind, the thought of frivolity surely follows. This concept of play is what anthropologists call galumphing. "We galumph when we hop instead of walk, when we take the scenic route instead of the efficient one, when we play a game whose rules demand a limitation of our powers, when we are interested in means rather than in ends. We voluntarily create obstacles and then enjoy overcoming them. In the higher animals and in people, it is of supreme evolutionary value" (Nachmanovitch 44). But huddled within the realm of play are science, math, music, art, language, history, and above all else, *engagement*. To play, the human brain must be engaged. To learn, the human brain must be engaged. To remember, the human brain must be engaged. The play suggested here, then, is play with purpose. Playing with words engages students and allows them to explore and interact with words in valuable ways. It gives words purpose. Without purpose, learning words becomes tedious and opportunities for retention are lessened.

"I think therefore I am," René Descartes famously observed in 1637. In 1994, Antonio Demasio revised this thought to "I *feel* therefore I am," in his book *Descartes' Error*, which explains the importance of emotion in human existence. I would like to extend this concept once more by adding, "I *play* therefore I am." What we are and how we feel are reflected in many areas of our brains. Playful thought helps develop these areas in meaningful ways. Without play, we would not have many of the ideas that we enjoy today.

Einstein might not have developed the theory of relativity. Mozart might not have composed *The Magic Flute*. Ford might never have envisioned the automobiles he designed. To play is to create; to create is to advance.

Like most areas of brain research, the idea of play is not novel. Cognitive psychologists such as Piaget and Lev Vygotsky have studied the impact and the importance of play for cognition. Not only does it enhance motivation, it actually creates better brains. In one science class, for example, students were asked to become molecules, and show the difference between solids, liquids, and gases. "As solids, they scrunched their bodies together, as liquids they moved freely in a limited space, and as gases they ran all over the room" (Von Oech 52). The importance of this activity, as far as the brain is concerned, lies in movement and play. Those kids will not soon forget the activity, or the difference between solids, gases, and liquids. When play is involved, the brain is happy; when the brain is happy, lasting neural connections are made.

Creativity in play also leads to many wonderful inventions. Sometimes play creates mistakes; sometimes those mistakes make people rich. "Some of the most important ideas were originally conceived for the purpose of play—their practical value to be discovered later" (Von Oech 90). Velcro, Post-It Notes, and many other moneymaking creations began as play, as "mistakes," or as serendipitous discoveries made in the process of exploration.

Play allows us to look at a subject in a different state of mind. We can explore topics under the influence of stress, anger, anxiety, and so forth, with little productivity. However, in the more relaxed mental state brought on by humor and playfulness, we take things more lightly, and ideas flow more easily. Good ideas, bad ideas, ludicrous ideas, extreme ideas, new ideas, old ideas—all come flowing out into the open for exploration. Under the influence of play, we can examine the madness before us. Yet in that madness, gold nuggets of creative possibility wait to be singled out or combined for that "Eureka effect," that "Ah-ha!" we have all experienced at some point.

Roger Von Oech observes that humor and play also allow us to put ideas together that typically would not be juxtaposed. Jokes that ask "What is the difference between…" or "What do X and Y have in common?" require the brain to make connections it would not normally make.

More than anything, humor and play are fun. Fun creates states of mind that are incredibly conducive to learning. Many people—including some educators—feel that learning is a mental discipline and that fun has little place in the classroom. "How sad, then, that we've turned the tables on nature and fostered a system of education that reinforces the opposite notion that learning only occurs when one is not having fun. Learning should just naturally be the most entertaining activity you can engage in—even if you are a law student studying for the Bar Exam" (Kline 7).

We must bring fun and play into our learning environments. Frivolity and a circus atmosphere is not the idea. Exploration, experimentation, and creativity, on the other hand, are the "stuff" learning is made from. As Peter Kline explains, "School should be the best party in town" (51).

The lessons shared in this chapter utilize playing with words and language in order to build and solidify vocabulary.

Nym Gym

Rationale:

Synonyms, antonyms, homonyms (homophones and homographs) enhance the complexity of the English language. The reason for this complexity stems from the history of the language and is explored in greater detail in Chapter Ten: Plugging in History.

Academic work, including vocabulary study, can be explored with a playful attitude. In schools we often hang on to the adage that "practice makes perfect." However, I once had a music teacher whose mantra was that practice only makes perfect if you practice perfectly. If skills are practiced out of context and without meaning, then practice will not make perfect. With imperfect practice, students will only be able to apply skills out of context, if at all; they may do their workbook pages perfectly, but may not be able to apply what they've been taught in any useful or meaningful way in their lives. Moreover, "if we split practice from the real thing, neither one of them will be very real. Through this split, many children have been irrevocably taught to hate piano or violin or music itself by the pedantic drill of oppressively boring exercises. Many others have been taught to hate literature, mathematics, or the very idea of productive work" (Nachmanovitch 67).

Students need more than the definition of *synonym, antonym, homonym,* and so forth. They need to understand why we have them, how we acquired them, and how they relate to each other and to other words in our language. They need to galumph and play a while with these words and the relationships between them through guided reflection, exploration, and ultimately creation. Nym Gym allows students to explore these relationships in a playful yet challenging manner.

Objective(s):

Students will understand the meaning of the terms *antonym, synonym, homonym, homograph,* and *homophone* (other -nyms optional). Likewise students will understand the difference between homonyms, homophones, and homographs. Words will be explored in a challenging puzzle format.

Materials:

-Nym Gym on transparency
-Read the poem "English is a Pain (Pane?)" by Shirlee Curlee Bingham, found in *No More Homework! No More Test!* Poems selected by Brian Lansky
-Optional: *I Love Lucy* episode "The Tutor"
-4 or more word dice (made with small wooden cubes from any craft store)

Presentation Guidelines:

- Read any selection that illustrates antonyms, synonyms, and/or homonyms. Possibilities are listed above.

- Explain that one reason the English language is so complex is because we have so many words for the same idea, numerous opposites for the same word, and then, incredibly challenging to all students, we have words that look the same, sound the same, or both, but actually mean something completely different. It is amazing that we are able to keep it all straight!

- Ask students if they know or can infer what the suffix -nym means. Hint that it sounds similar to what it actually means (-nym = name). Use every opportunity to make students aware of affixes and how they affect the meaning of words.
  Antonym–Names that are opposite (happy/sad; concrete/abstract)
  Synonym–Names that are the same (tired/exhausted; tiny/infinitesimal)
  Homonyms–Names that are spelled and sound the same but mean something different (*walk*, verb; and *walk*, noun)
  Homograph–Words that look the same but have different pronunciations and meanings (*wound*, an injury; and *wound*, as in "coiled")
  Homophone–Words that sound alike but look different and have a different meaning (*to, two, too*)

- Place a chart on the board and ask students to brainstorm as many examples as possible.
  NOTE: Brainstorming poses the danger of only involving a few students. I now utilize what I call **3/5/10 brainstorming**. Students should each come up with **three** of each type of -nym by themselves. I tell them this is a solo moment. This gives all students an opportunity to think and explore possibilities. Students

should then share their answers with students sitting around them. As a group, students should be able to come up with **five** possibilities for each type of word. Now students can blend ideas, borrow ideas, and clarify possible misunderstandings before blurting something out that will cause embarrassment. This provides safety for less secure students. Finally, students are truly ready to brainstorm as a class. Now all students have been engaged in the process at one level or another. The class should suggest **ten** words for each of the three types of -nyms.

- Show the transparency of the -Nym Gym Chart. Explain that the challenge is to roll one die, begin with that word, and then add words to reach the twelfth box. Each word added must be connected to the previous word by being an antonym, a synonym, or a homonym (homograph or homophone).

- Students must show the relationship between the words by writing *antonym, synonym,* or *homonym, homograph,* or *homophone* on the shadowed line between the boxes.

- The part of speech should be included for each word in the bottom right-hand corner. This is important for homonyms because they look and sound alike. It is the usage that separates them.

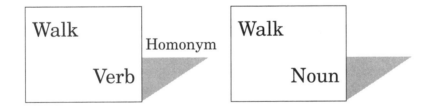

- Model by sharing the following completed example, pointing out the relationship between the words as you go.

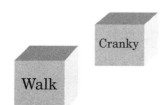

-Nym Gym

Word Workout for Mental Muscles

Cranky · Tired · Walk · Think

Directions: Roll one of the four word dice. Write the word you (or your team) rolled in the first box. Each word you add must be a homonym (include homographs and homophones), synonym, or antonym to the word directly before. Example: Your first word is WALK (v). The next word can be RUN (antonym), or WALK (n) (homonym), or STROLL (synonym). Your challenge is to fill all twelve squares following this pattern. The form of the word can change (present to past tense, etc.) as long as the word you write is one of Them -Nyms! On the shadow line, write the type of connection used between the two words: Homonym (homograph, homophone), Synonym, or Antonym.

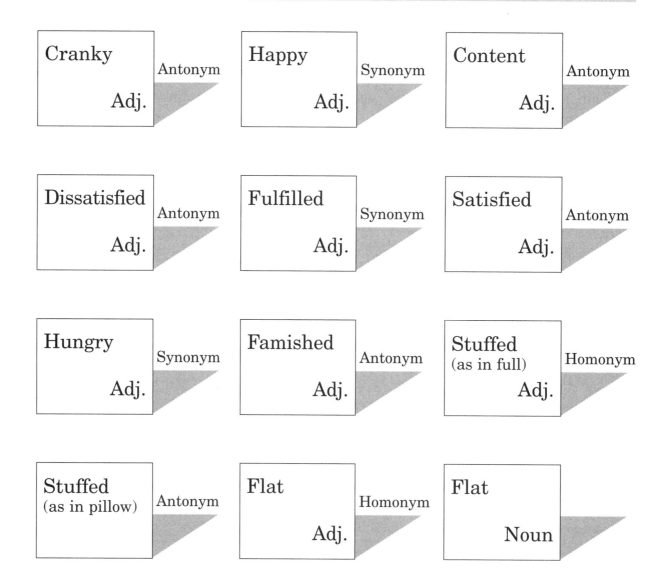

Cranky Adj. — *Antonym*	**Happy** Adj. — *Synonym*	**Content** Adj. — *Antonym*
Dissatisfied Adj. — *Antonym*	**Fulfilled** Adj. — *Synonym*	**Satisfied** Adj. — *Antonym*
Hungry Adj. — *Synonym*	**Famished** Adj. — *Antonym*	**Stuffed** (as in full) Adj. — *Homonym*
Stuffed (as in pillow) — *Antonym*	**Flat** Adj. — *Homonym*	**Flat** Noun

Example from Kara Rose and Lisa Edwards
Aldine ISD; Houston, Texas

You are an awesome Nym Wit!

- For guided practice, complete one -Nym Gym Chart as a class, in teams, or in pairs.
- Using a dictionary, a thesaurus, or other resources is suggested, at least initially. Most students are not at a point where they are able to pull -nyms out of their heads. The use of resources will also encourage them to seek higher-level words.
- Once students are secure with the procedures and processes for -Nym Gym, they are ready to try one on their own for study or assessment purposes.

Evaluation/Variation(s):

- **Possible Point Scale:**

Words	3 points
Connections between words	3 points
Part of speech	2 points
Antonym used	2 points if one is used
Synonym used	2 points if one is used
Homonym	2 points if one is used
(homograph, homophone)	1 point if one is used

- Extra points might be given for three-syllable or larger words
- Words can come from a novel or story that students are currently reading. (Warning: not all words work as easily as others.)
- Give students a list of bonus words. Extra points are given if the word(s) appear in any of the 12 boxes.

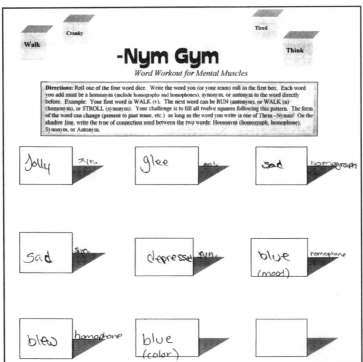

6th grade -Nym Gym sample. Students do not have to reach the end to benefit from the workout!

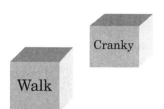

-Nym Gym

Word Workout for Mental Muscles

Directions: Roll one of the four word dice. Write the word you (or your team) rolled in the first box. Each word you add must be a homonym (include homographs and homophones), synonym, or antonym to the word directly before. Example: Your first word is WALK (v). The next word can be RUN (antonym), or WALK (n) (homonym), or STROLL (synonym). Your challenge is to fill all twelve squares following this pattern. The form of the word can change (present to past tense, etc.) as long as the word you write is one of Them -Nyms! On the shadow line, write the type of connection used between the two words: Homonym (homograph, homophone), Synonym, or Antonym. Challenge yourself to use all of Them -Nyms!

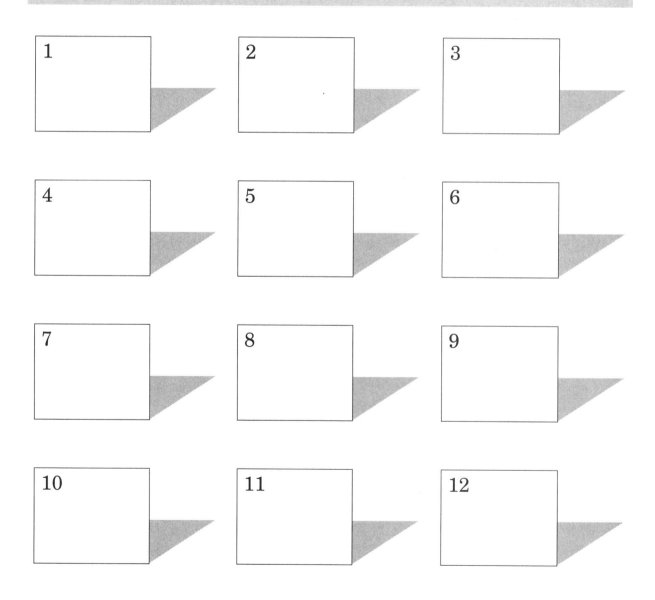

You are an awesome Nym Wit!

Them-Nyms
Other -Nyms Worth Naming!
-nym: *from Greek, meaning word or name*

ano**nym**ous	having no name	An anonymous donor
acronym	initials of other words	N.A.S.A., F.B.I., C.I.A
anatonym	part of the body used as a verb	toe the line, face the music
aptronym	name especially suited to profession	John Couch: furniture salesman; Emily Baker: pastry shop owner
autonym	a word that describes itself	Hippopotomonstrosesquipedalian: "pertaining to a very long word"
capitonym	a word that changes meaning and pronunciation when it is capitalized	Herb; herb
charactonym	name of a literary character whose name matches the character's personality	J. K. Rowling is a master of this with the Harry Potter series. Dudley Malfoy Snape and many, many more!
contronym	words that evolve to have two polar meanings	bad (awful) then became bad (awesome)
eponym	"after or upon a name" (words that come from the names of people or places)	Jeep, Chap Stick, Levi's
exonym	a place name used by foreigners that is different from the name used by natives	Cologne for Köln, Germany
heteronym (special form of homograph)	spelled the same but have different pronunciation and meaning	read, read lead, lead resume, resume
holonym	a concept that has another concept as a part	door is a holonym of knob
hyponym	a word whose meaning denotes a subordinate	a dog is a hyponym of animal
meronym	a term midway between two opposites	convex, flat, and concave
metonym	a name that stands for something in which it is closely related	crown in reference to the monarchy
pseudonym	false name	Dr. Seuss, Mark Twain, Eminem
retronym	adjective-noun pairing generated by a change in the meaning of the noun	bottled water rather than simply water
tautonym	a word composed of two identical parts	Tutu, goody-goody, tom-tom

Making Sense of the Differences

HOMONYMS Same Name (LOOK) Same SOUND (Truly multiple meaning words)		HOMOPHONES Same SOUND Different LOOK		HOMOGRAPHS (Heteronyms) Same LOOK Different SOUND (often due to location of stressed syllable; typically a noun/verb pairing)	
Walk (V)	Walk (N)	Foul	Fowl	InCENSE	INcense
Run (V)	Run (N)	Cite	Sight	ConTENT	CONtent
Touch (V)	Touch (N)	Gait	Gate	INvalid	InVALID
Flat (Adj)	Flat (N)	Base	Bass	CONtest	ConTEST
Attack (V)	Attack (N)	Cent	Scent	House	House
Picture (V)	Picture (N)	Cereal	Serial	Excuse	Excuse
Map (V)	Map (N)	Knows	Nose	Dove	Dove
Number (V)	Number (N)	Weak	Week	Record	Record
Name (V)	Name (N)	Throne	Thrown	Present	Present
Bottle (V)	Bottle (N)	Sew	So	Polish	Polish
Right (Adj.)	Right (N)	See	Sea	Produce	Produce
Fair (Adj.)	Fair (N)	Suite	Sweet	Project	Project
Drink (V)	Drink (N)	Role	Roll	Wind	Wind
Cross (V)	Cross (N)	Plain	Plane	Sow	Sow
Glass (Adj.)	Glass (N)	Rye	Wry	Subject	Subject
Seat (V)	Seat (N)	Wring	Ring	Secreted	Secreted
Anger (V)	Anger (N)	None	Nun	Separate	Separate
Page (V)	Page (N)	Moan	Mown	Tear	Tear
Call (V)	Call (N)	Moose	Mousse	Live	Live
Commute (V)	Commute (N)	Mail	Male	Console	Console
Record (Adj.)	Record (N)	Him	Hymn	Bow	Bow
Test (V)	Test (N)	Heal	Heel	August	August
Tune (V)	Tune (N)	Hall	Haul	Alternate	Alternate
Heat (V)	Heat (N)	Creak	Creek	Close	Close

 Vocabulary Unplugged • ©2005 Alana Morris • www.discoverwriting.com

Word Spins

Rationale:

I love it when new gadgets or products hit the market. Nothing can motivate me more to clean the house than the appearance of a new cleanser or some other new cleaning product to make the job simpler. But at the same time, there are certain products and tools I have used for years that I would never trade for the latest model. I sometimes need the new for the motivation and to raise my attention level; I need the old for reliability and structure. If everything I had was new, I would spend more time playing and trying to figure things out, and would get little actual cleaning done.

The same balance between old and new is needed within our classrooms. Ritual or standard ways of doing things create a certain security in the environment. "The problem is the brain downshifts in excessively unruly and unpredictable conditions or, for that matter, when there are few borders and too many choices. It also downshifts under coercion and threat. Creative teaching cannot flourish in total chaos" (Caine 151). Actually, the more ritual there is within the structure of a classroom, the more novelty the teacher can include. If novelty is used all of the time, then the novelty becomes ritual. It sounds like a paradox—but the point is that as teachers we need to determine the successful balance between the unpredictable that gets our students' attention and the predictable that gives them something secure to hang on to.

When we've used ritual to create a classroom comfort zone, then we've made a space to introduce novelty. It is novelty that lures the reticular system within the brain to pay attention, and only when attention is activated can information be processed into long term memory. "Attention, then, must remain centered in dynamic tension between distraction and obsession if our behavior is to stay on a moderate course" (Hobson 167). All of our senses love the intrigue of something new: a new scent, a new scene on the side of the road, a new texture on a delicate fabric, a new sound from an unusual source, or a new appetizer at our favorite restaurant that beckons us to the edge of our seats to ask, "What is *that*?" The brain wants to know and we seek the answer because it is new. "Since the brain isn't designed to attend to ALL types of incoming stimuli, it sorts out that which is less critical to our survival. Any stimuli introduced into our immediate environment which is either new (novel) or of sufficiently different emotional intensity (high contrast) will immediately get our attention" (Jensen [1996] 166).

Hobson further explains that attention is state dependent. Simply telling or asking someone to pay attention is not likely to elicit the behavior we want. As the designers of the lessons, we must know what catches the human brain's attention, and we must not attempt to hold it for too long. We have to get the attention, set the motivation for receiving the information, and then we must know how to get out of the way and allow processing and reflection to occur. The best way to capitalize on the brain's attention system is to turn the learning over to the student. When students are actively engaged, the attention is automatically there, and the teacher does not have to compete against all of the stimuli directed toward the brain.

A couple of years ago, while waiting in line at a department store, I saw a stack of CDs for installing a popular Internet browser. The sign said "Take One." My mind first reflected on the massive promotional bombardment practiced by this company, but quickly moved to "Don't mind if I do." In fact I took more than one—which my then six-year-old daughter immediately pointed out. I explained that I had taken one for each person who would need one for my next staff training.

That stack of CDs gave me an idea for how this advertising tool could be used as a teaching resource. Once again, novelty doesn't often come from the chapters of the text-book. Novelty comes from seeing what others see in a different light. The newness of that moment gets the brain's attention and facilitates learning.

Objective(s):

Students will explore and create Word Spins in order to examine patterns of language such as syllables, affixes, sound patterns, parts of speech, rhyming words, and so forth.

Materials:

CDs (used or unused)
**These can be acquired free from numerous sources such as old textbook adoptions, companies that send them in the mail or give them away, computer stores, etc. Be creative; they are everywhere.
Dice for center
Alphabet stickers
Permanent markers
Rulers (optional)

Presentation Guidelines:

- Show students a few Word Spins that have been created.
- Making a Word Spin:
    1. Take a blank CD.
    2. Use a ruler and a permanent marker to divide the CD into eight relatively equal parts.
    3. Decide what concept your Word Spin will focus on. (Example: syllables)

4. There are at least two ways to create Word Spins that focus on syllables. Place one word in each of the eight segments. The words should vary in length.

5. When the student spins the disk on his or her finger, the word where the finger points is the target word. The student must then tell how many syllables are in that word. The partner will agree or disagree and the spins continue.

6. A second way to focus on syllables and to vacuum up word residue, is to use the Alphabet Word Spins for syllables.

7. Using alphabet stickers of any variety, place one letter in each of the eight segments. I make three Word Spins with one set of alphabet stickers. Some letters can be left off (X, Z, Q).

8. This is where the die comes in. The student will roll the die and then spin the Word Spin. If the number was 4 and the letter was N, the student will give a four-syllable word that begins with N. I always have a dictionary and timer available. Students can have one minute to find a word, if they wish.

9. Students keep score by securing points based on the number of syllables rolled and correct answers (a three syllable word earns the student 3 points).

Sample Prefix Word Spin

- **Word Spin Directions**–I like to place the directions on a CD as follows:

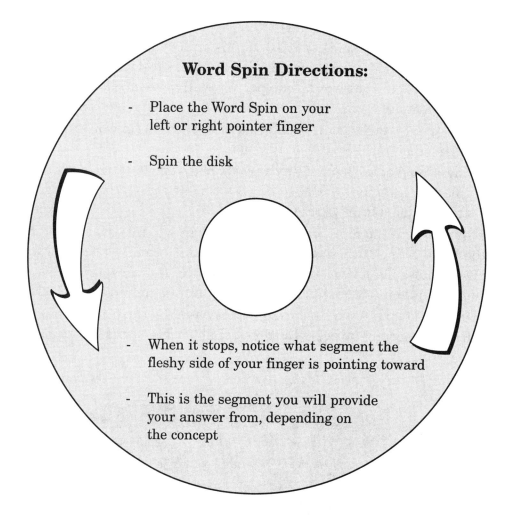

Word Spin Directions:

- Place the Word Spin on your left or right pointer finger

- Spin the disk

- When it stops, notice what segment the fleshy side of your finger is pointing toward

- This is the segment you will provide your answer from, depending on the concept

- After exploring the Word Spins, students should work with a partner or alone to create their own Word Spin.
- Word Spins are designed to explore words and language. As discussed in Chapter One: Plugging in Memory, opportunities to vacuum up the residue of words are important for retention.
- Use the syllable Word Spin to model the procedure and process.

Evaluation/Variation(s):

- Grades may be given for the creation of a Word Spin. A rubric will be the ideal way to grade the product.
- Answers for the Word Spins can be written down. Student can be given grades for these answers. The developmental level of your students will determine how many words are required for each spin and the point system used.
- A numerical grade does not have to be taken. Often the peer feedback and wordplay is sufficient.

Possible Word Spins

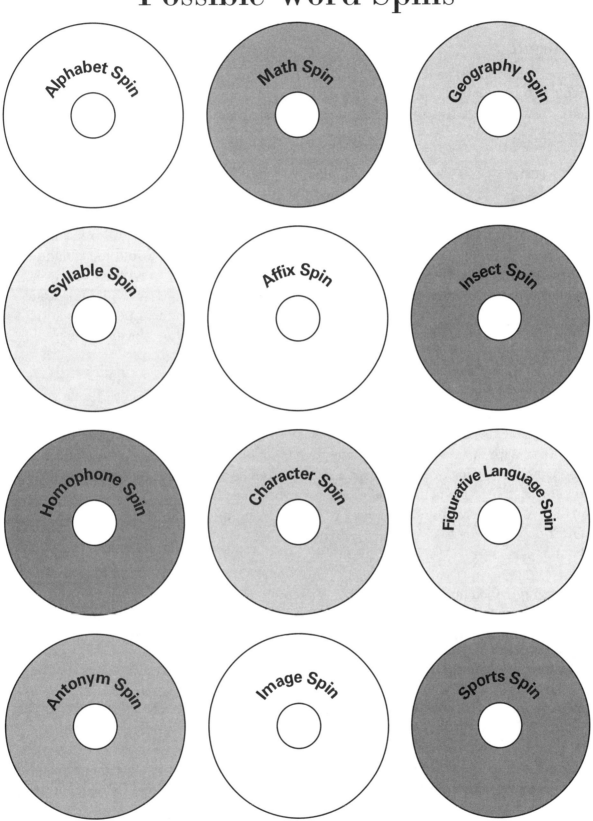

Wordplay Play

Rationale:

"Reading, counting, speaking, and problem solving are all maturation correlated. And it's play that speeds the process. It does it faster and more efficiently than other means because play usually has the recipe for brain growth built in: challenge, novelty, feedback, and time" (Jensen /*Learning with the Brain* 76).

Play is certainly not "fluff," as some believe. Play is creative work that solidifies and synthesizes what we know. "Creative work is play; it is free speculation using the materials of one's chosen form. The creative mind plays with objects it loves. Artists play with color and space, musicians play with sound and silence...Children play with everything they can get their hands on" (Nachmanovitch 42). I would like to add that readers and writers of all ages and levels play with words. By playing with words through dramatic play, students are able to synthesize and solidify what they know about language and the world. Such synthesis strengthens neural pathways and increases the potential for retention and higher-level vocabulary development.

Since my daughter was old enough to speak we have played a game based on the book *I Love You, Goodnight* by Jon Buller and Susan Schade. I will tell her, "I love you more than the rain loves falling." She will respond back with something like "I love you more than pickles love green." We play this affectionate word game, trying to outdo each other with our response, until we give up or fall asleep. She is now eight and the game continues. However, her responses are often so thoughtful and high-level that they surprise me. Responses such as "I love you more than a mirror loves reflection," and "I love you more than books love words," remind me of the importance of such mental play and the true brilliance of children that is often not illuminated in some school experiences.

Interestingly enough, the pattern Eric Jensen shared in 2001 in his book *Learning with the Brain in Mind* continues. The 2002 profile of college-bound students released by the College Board indicates that students with experience in acting or play production outscored students with no such course work by 66 points on the verbal portion of the SAT Exam (College Board 2002). Playing, like reading and writing, is a mode of learning.

Objective(s):

Students will explore and review their knowledge of learned wordplay by performing a short (three- to five-minute) play. Content knowledge or synthesis of a novel or story will be used as the subject matter for the play.

Materials:

-List of Word Play options
-Props can be provided by the students and/or the teacher
-Rubric for scoring the production

Presentation Guidelines:

- Show a clip of a movie or commercial that uses wordplay. The possibilities are endless. Some textbooks even have Viewing and Representing components that can be used.
- Copyright note: If only a brief clip is being used for nonprofit educational use, the viewing falls under "fair use" guidelines.
- Explain that wordplay grabs the brain's attention and provides humor and novelty. Further discuss the fact that comedians rely on wordplay to make a living.
- As a way to examine their knowledge of vocabulary, language, and wordplay, explain that they will be placed in groups of three to five students for the assignment.
- The groups will:
  —Create a three- to five-minute skit, commercial, sitcom, original movie scene, etc.
  —The subject matter will be content based (math, science, history, music, P.E., etc.) or may be focused around a current novel or story being read.
  —A minimum of five different wordplay techniques will be included for full credit.
- SEE *NOW PLAYING* LESSON INTRODUCTION PAGE

Evaluation/Variations:

- A rubric should be used to score this brief production. Components that may be included:
  —Five wordplay techniques
  —Script (including score for conventions of language)
  —Props
  —Clarity of speech
  —Preparation
- Each teacher will have unique ideas and objectives. The assessment, however, should match the instruction and the objectives.
- Possible wordplay options to include in the production (just a sampling):
  —alliteration
  —puns
  —homonyms
  —antonyms
  —synonyms
  —other -nyms
  —Tom Swifties ("I've struck oil," said Tom crudely. "I love pancakes," said Tom flippantly.)
  —Extended metaphor
  —Joke (must match content and timing)

"All the world is a stage."
    –Shakespeare

Now Playing!

Words For A Brainy Day!

A Series of Short Plays Illuminating the Playful, yet
Complex Nature of the English Language

FEATURING:

Five or more wordplay possibilities

A script written by all members of the 3–5-person cast

Well-planned, well-practiced, well-delivered lines

Content area subject matter

OR

**Synthesized information from a novel you have read
this year**

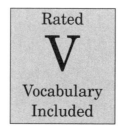

Rated

V

Vocabulary
Included

Anguish Languish (English Language)

Rationale:

By exploring this specific type of wordplay, students can see how the sounds of words bring a variety of meanings, and can use a wide assortment of words in the process. This form of wordplay is easier for students who have a large storehouse of words. However, it should be thought of as an exploration, which with guided practice can introduce even the novice wordsmith to numerous new words.

Objective(s):

Students will explore words and the sounds of word patterns through a form of word pun.

Following the guidelines originally set forth by Professor Howard L. Chance, students will replace words from an original text with words that are similar but not exactly the same in sound (Lederer [1996] 77). This fun form of punning is briefly explained in the introduction to this chapter ("Wordplay: No Bling Bling Required"). Nursery rhymes are most commonly used; however, song lyrics work well and are incredibly engaging for most students.

Presentation Guidelines:

- Model the technique carefully before turning students loose (or lose) with the concept.
- Have them try to translate these titles shared by Richard Lederer in *Puns and Games*:
  -"Ladle Rat Rotten Hut"
  -"Guilty Looks Enter Tree Boars"
  -"Oiled Mortar Harbored"
  (*Little Red Riding Hood, Goldilocks and the Three Bears,* and *Old Mother Hubbard*)
- Once students understand how the process works, allow them to try it out with a partner. Have them put any form of text into Anguish Languish format. Remind students that all of the words they use have to be real words. They cannot simply misspell the original word.
- Have a sharing time in which students can read their creative language play out loud. The brain sees one thing until the ears get involved. Then the meaning comes to life.

Evaluation/Variations:

- This word exploration game works well in a language center.
- Ask students to summarize the main part of a novel chapter in Anguish Languish format. The neurons will certainly be firing! This synthesizes information at an incredibly high level.
- Scoring should be determined based on the objectives set forth by each individual teacher.
- Feedback is most critical on a language endeavor such as Anguish Languish.

Chapter 3
Plugging In Movement

"Movement is the door to learning."

–Paul E. Denison

When asked to recall phone numbers, I often have to hold out an imaginary phone and "air-dial" the number to retrieve it from memory. Likewise, orally spelling words requires the same kinesthetic activity: I must get out a pen and paper to accurately spell difficult words asked of me by students and/or peers. Obviously, both my body and my mind are essential to the task required. Trying to determine which is more important is like asking a master violinist if the right hand or the left hand is most essential. They both work together to make music.

In the same way, the body and mind work together to make learning happen. Often this comes about through movement. "Movement is a basic human experience. It heralds life inside the womb, and it becomes an expression of need and intent once the child is born. The experience of the self, and all that immediately surrounds a youngster, is linked to children's explorations of both" (John-Steiner 13). An infant's movements indeed show both need and intent. Such gestures are early forms of communication. Movement is basic to both communication and learning, though it is often excluded from classroom lessons.

"We build up our brain-mind maps by incorporating the results of exploring the environment and moving through it, while at the same time sniffing it, hearing it, and feeling its textures" (Hobson 144). Our students must experience our classrooms in this same manner. We now have new understandings into the cerebellum areas of the brain and their role in memory storage. Many areas of the brain are involved in movement, but the cerebellum is a key region. Many of our most important memories are localized in this area as well. It is the cerebellum that tells the body to quickly duck out of the way when a heavy, dangerous object is thrown in its direction. If we had to wait for the neocortex—the reasoning area of the brain—to "think" about what it is supposed to do in such a situation, our emergency rooms would be constantly overflowing with ongoing tragedies.

    Physiologically, we know that memories are stored throughout the brain, not just in the thalamus and cortex. We also know that the body has its own kind of memory as well. It is our body that receives and then rehearses much of the information we encounter each day. We receive this information through our skin and other sensory receptors. The sense of touch is often overlooked but is also essential to experiencing the world.

"As the body receives and interprets thousands of bits of information every second, infinitesimal adjustments are made in our chemistry and subtle muscular and neuronal shifts take place remote from our awareness" (Houston 2). In other words, the brain literally changes at the chemical level when our mind and/or body experience something new. These changes have important implications for learning. When we understand the key role the body plays in learning and encourage our students to explore the possibilities of movement, it can only enhance their learning. Students are likely to be actively engaged when they are moving; this engagement sparks learning.

The old paradigm, under which movement has generally been frowned upon in schools, is outdated, as Dr. Jean Houston notes. "The active, indeed the wriggling, child's body is urged to 'sit still,' to restrain its natural impetus toward movement and exploration as it is confined to chair and school desk that always seem to be designed for someone else. Under these circumstances, the discomforts of the body are best relegated to the unconscious, and the forgetting, the sleeping, begins" (3). By finding ways to allow movement in learning, particularly in learning words, we increase students' engagement and thereby their ability to retain and use new words. The lessons offered in this chapter provide a way for students to wriggle and learn at the same time.

Psyche (mind) and soma (body) can no longer be viewed as separate regions that are each controlled and manipulated by the other; they are intricately woven together like the silk strands on a weaver's loom. They work together to create, explore, and ultimately learn. By taking advantage of this knowledge, our students can remember at levels they may not have experienced previously. "The body is more than simply another machine, indistinguishable from the artificial objects of the world. It is also the vessel of the individual's sense of self, his most personal feelings and aspirations, as well as that entity in which others respond in a special way because of their uniquely human qualities" (Gardner 235). The importance of the self and the learner's sense of self has been extensively explored and documented in the research on learning.

There is no greater connection than that between the human body and the human mind. Actors remember their lines by acting them out, not by sitting in a chair and reading them. Astronauts rehearse what they are to experience in space through simulation, not by sitting and reading about it. CPR classes, thank goodness, are taught using models for participants to practice on, not by having learners merely read through the step-by-step procedures.

Our society is ferociously competing to disseminate information. Unfortunately, though a computer can store this mass of data, our brains are not designed to do so as discussed in Chapter One. If we want to be able to process and store even a small fraction of the incoming information, we have to let the brain work in the most effective manner possible. Bringing the body and movement into the learning episode is an important part of the process.

Soma in Motion
(Body in Motion)

Rationale:

One of the problems with vocabulary study is that students often do not truly internalize the concept of the word they have learned. They simply memorize the definition and the one or two sentences given or created as examples. Often the examples provided do not fit into the schema of the student's world. My middle school age son is tested on over twenty vocabulary words each week. Most of these words he has no investment in and will memorize just long enough for the test—then go back to using the words that he "owns" because they have become part of his knowing. If students are going to be required to know words from random lists prescribed by outside sources—workbooks, textbook-generated lists, programs purchased by schools, etc.—then we must exert the energy necessary to allow students to explore the words in meaningful ways. As discussed in Chapter One: Plugging in Memory, we must help students find connections to prior knowledge of concepts and words so that the new information has an opportunity to be fully absorbed, rather than simply memorized for the sake of a weekly test.

Objective:

Students will explore new or less familiar words using movement.

Materials:

List of words to be learned
Index cards

Presentation Guidelines:

- Share with students that our senses are incredibly important for making memories solid.
- Ask students to share senses that impact memory. Possible responses:
                    smell   taste   sound   vision   touch
- Suggest to students that movement builds memories as well. See if they can come up with strong memories tied to movement.
- Explain that movement is an excellent way to build solid memories of vocabulary words.
- Share with students that *psyche* is the root word for mind, and *soma* is the root word for body. Therefore, the strategy Soma in Motion uses the body and movement to help the brain remember words.

- Share the following example (or another example you devise):

  Word: *Expunge*

  Meaning: to wipe out, obliterate, erase

  Movement: Take your hand and act like you are wiping something off of your left, upper arm.

- Be sure to explain to the students that the definition is not given when they share their word. Only the word and the movement are shared in the early stage of the process.

- Once you have modeled taking a word, internalizing the definition, and then providing a movement that clearly illustrates the meaning, then do another example as a class.

- Give students the word *incubate* (any word can be given, depending on the age and level of the students).

- Ask one student to look the word up in the dictionary. There are numerous dictionary websites that make this process incredibly fast.

- Ask students to brainstorm possible movements that would clearly "show" the meaning of *incubate* (or whichever word is selected).

- Choose one of the recommended movements and then have students say the word incubate and then demonstrate the movement. Saying the word is important to assist in accurate pronunciation.

- Though at this point you have only modeled two words, you can show the students how the assessment will work.

- For the assessment, only the definition is given. You will say "What word means to wipe off or erase?" You can make the movement as a reminder. Students should all respond that expunge is the accurate answer.

- This will give the students an idea of the full process. Obviously there will be more words once the whole class creates their movements. The class assessment is not oral; the answers are written on paper. After you give each definition and the reminder movement, students will write the corresponding word on their own papers.

- Once students understand the process, give each pair of students a word on an index card. Two options are available:

- The definition may already be provided, or students can be asked to look up the definition.

- The decision is based on the objectives of the lesson. If dictionary skills are not part of the objectives for the lesson, then it is far better to provide the definition.

- Provide time for each pair to create an appropriate movement for their word (approximately ten minutes). Be sure to monitor carefully during this creation stage in case some of the movements are not clear or do not match the definition.

- After the ten-minute creation time, ask students to get in a large circle and stay with their partner(s).

- Each pair will say their word and the rest of the class will repeat the word. Again, it is important that any errors in pronunciation be corrected before the movement is given. Student pairs will say the word again as they are demonstrating the movement.
- After each pair has shared their word and movement, review all of the words and movements in a random order.

5th grade students at Stehlik Intermediate in Houston, Texas showing scintilla.

5th grade students at Stehlik Intermediate in Houston, Texas showing intrepid.

Evaluation/ Variations:

- The assessment of the words is actually something to look forward to because the students discover how many words they have learned in a relatively short amount of time.
- Have the words randomly listed on the board or on a transparency. At this point, we are still scaffolding accurate spelling. It is important that students are able to see the words.
- Students should number their papers according to the number of words learned.
- The teacher will provide only the definition (and possibly the movement) for each word. After hearing the definition, students will write the appropriate matching word. Again, students are easily able to match the definition with the words and movements they have rehearsed.
- The teacher will decide what type of grade should be taken on this first go-around.
- This type of vocabulary study is incredibly successful because it involves many areas of the brain. Ongoing review and rehearsal will further strengthen the understanding and memory of the words. Lunch duty and hall duty are wonderful opportunities for review. I will see a student and do one of the animated movements—it never fails to bring a huge grin and a ready and accurate definition and/or word in response.
- The strategy is wonderful for content area words and allows the words to be reviewed in all classes.
- Eventually the movements are not required for review as students more deeply internalize the words and *own* their meaning and context.

Having a Ball with Vocabulary

Rationale:

Most educators would agree on the importance of students' learning prefixes, suffixes, roots, and patterns, in general, for word study. But how to study these numerous components of the English language is of greater importance than if or why. Once again, movement is a valuable tool to use for solidifying information and enhancing memory formation. This hands-on strategy allows students to experience vocabulary and word knowledge in a kinesthetic fashion. The play associated with the activity increases both motivation and memory for the details of the language.

Objective:

Students will practice prefixes, suffixes, and root words in an interactive game that practices, reviews, and assesses students' knowledge of these critical language components.

Materials:

A plain, round ball (large size)
4 permanent markers (red, green, brown, and black)
A detailed list of prefixes, suffixes, and root words (*The Reading Teacher's Book of Lists 3rd Edition* by Fry, et al. has the most comprehensive list I have come across)

Presentation Guidelines:

* The ball must be created prior to utilizing the strategy. The teacher (or older student helpers) will draw a grid around the surface of the ball. Lines should circle completely around the ball, both horizontally and vertically.

  Hint: Every rubber ball has a small seam line around the ball. This is the perfect guide for creating the first straight line around the ball. After drawing the first line, continue to add new lines about one inch below the previously drawn line in a parallel pattern. Once all of the horizontal lines are completed, rotate the ball and begin the same process creating lines that are perpendicular to the first set of lines.

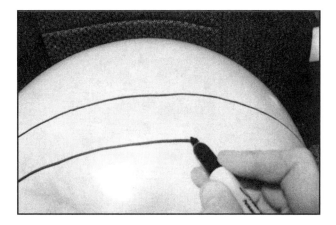

- Once the lines have been drawn, there should be numerous rectangles that have been created. Within each of the boxes, you will write either a root, a prefix, or a suffix using the following color-code:

Prefixes	Green	Memory Hook: Green connects with go or start, which reminds students that prefixes are at the beginning or the start of the word.
Suffixes	Red	Memory Hook: Red connects with stop or end, which reminds students that suffixes are at the end of the word.
Root Words	Brown	Memory Hook: Brown connects with the earth or ground where roots grow, which reminds students that the roots are the core of the words.

The colors help the students know what they are being asked throughout the process of the game. It also assists the brain in organizing the information for memory. The ball is ready for play once all of the rectangles are full. Repeating more common prefixes, suffixes, and roots within the grid will be necessary to fill all of the spaces.

Playing the Game:

- Students should be divided into two or more teams. I have discovered an important strategy for making the teams more effective in an academic game such as this. Invisible teams are my favorite. I place students into teams before they come to class (see Invisible Team Monitor Chart on page 50). The teams are invisible because students do not know, until the end of the game, who is on their team. I typically place four to five students on each team. This encourages students to not yell out answers because they do not know if they are giving the answer to an opposing team member. The greatest benefit of invisible teams is it allows everyone to celebrate successes and not be critical of errors.

- I use the Invisible Team Monitor Chart to keep up with and monitor which affixes have been utilized in the game and which student receives or is denied the point for his or her answer. No matter what, the correct answer is provided before the game proceeds.

- Students should arrange themselves into a large circle (outside, a gym area, the cafeteria, a foyer, etc., tend to work best to play the game).

- I model the game by asking a student to toss me the ball. I ask this student to call out my name prior to throwing the ball. It is important that students call out the name of the person to whom they are tossing the ball. Otherwise, students may not be prepared and could be hit in the face.

- I catch the ball firmly with both hands. I show students that I will be focusing on where my right thumb lands when I catch the ball.

  Example: If the right thumb lands on the root word *morte*, the student would say that the root means "death." I also ask the students to provide an example such as "mortuary." Sometimes it is easier for a student to provide the example first. This primes the brain by providing a context prior to retrieving an isolated definition.

- It is okay for the students (and the teacher) not to know every answer. Always have the list of affixes used on the ball so the accurate answers can be provided or checked as needed. The first few times you play, correct answers will have to be given often.

- Once the game starts, the receiving student attempts to answer and then chooses the next student to receive the ball.
- It is important that all feedback is positive and helps students learn whichever affix is in question. I try to provide memory hooks or examples to help when students do not know the answer. All students are encouraged to listen carefully because the chances are good that the word part will come up again during the game.
- This process continues until as many students as possible have had a turn. Initially, the game will take more time because students may not know too many of the answers. As students get better with their knowledge of affixes, less clarification and time is needed.

Evaluation/Variations:

- Playing the game is part of the guided practice in order to scaffold students toward greater mastery of word parts. Though a grade can be given for the game, it is not essential. The feedback is the most critical element during the guided practice.
- After playing the game, however, accountability and evaluation are important. Leave enough time at the close of the game for a quick ten-minute assessment.
- I use the Invisible Team Monitor Chart to select five to ten of the affixes to assess, which were discussed during the game.
- There are many options for this quick check:
  - give an example of the definition and ask students to provide the affix
  - give the affix and ask students to provide an example and/or the definition
  - Splash Down Assessment: Ask students to write down at least five of the affixes they learned that day, providing the definition and an example. I also ask that each student give one affix where the definition is unclear.
- The variations for this activity are endless. Rather than affixes, any concept can be practiced and monitored through this game process (parts of speech, plot elements, poetry devices, history, math, science, music terms, and so forth).
- The ball itself serves as a portable Word Wall. Whenever it is placed in the room, students will be able to look at it and mentally review the affixes or other concepts.

Invisible Team Monitor Chart

Students Team A	Affix	Example -/+	Definition -/+
Students Team B	Affix	Example -/+	Definition -/+
Students Team C	Affix	Example -/+	Definition -/+
Students Team D	Affix	Example -/+	Definition -/+
Students Team E	Affix	Example -/+	Definition -/+
Students Team F	Affix	Example -/+	Definition -/+

 Vocabulary Unplugged • ©2005 Alana Morris • www.discoverwriting.com

Syllable Squat

Rationale:

Knowing the importance of movement for learning, I originally developed this exercise while working with second-grade students. Syllable divisions and the understanding of the concept of syllables is abstract for all students. Rather than employing small movements (such as jaw movements) to indicate a new syllable, the Syllable Squat uses large muscle movements to clearly define for learners where words divide into syllables.

Objectives:

Using words generated by the teacher and/or the class, students will use their legs, bending at the knee, to move down and back up, repeating the movements based on the number of syllables.

Materials:

Index cards or other paper for students to generate words
Teacher-generated list of words, if needed

Presentation Guidelines:

- Share with students the importance of syllables for spelling and pronunciation.

produce vs. produce

The syllable placement in pronunciation determines whether the word is a noun or a verb.

- Model how, by dividing words such as *exaggerate* into syllables, we can more easily achieve accurate spelling.

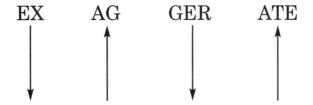

Without the syllable divisions, students (even adults) often misspell *exaggerate* as *exagerate*.

- The teacher will first model the syllable squat process.

Example: If I use the word *pizza*, I will squat down and say "PIZ," and then when I return to the standing position, I will say "ZA."

PIZ-   -ZA

- Ask students to suggest various words to continue to model. Ask all of the students to stand and continue taking word suggestions, which the teacher and the class then *squat*.
- Once students understand the Syllable Squat process, they are ready for more advanced squatting as a class and independently.

Evaluation/Variations:

- Evaluation through grades is not needed for the Syllable Squat; it is a strategy to enhance spelling and to provide movement when needed to change emotional and attention mental states.
- As a warm-up, ask students to generate words from a lesson they had the previous day (from your class or another content area). Gather the words and use them for a nice squat variation I call Syllable Squat Olympics. Each table or group of students will squat the words from the student-generated collection as you call them out (up to five words for each table). The groups get a point for each of the five words they accurately squat in a completely synchronized fashion. If anyone stays up when he or she should be down or vice versa, then move on to the next group. The table(s) or group(s) with the most points reigns as the Syllable Squat Champs (may be more than one group) until the next opportunity for the Olympics rolls around.
- Utilize the Syllable Squat prior to Soma in Motion for pre-exposure to the words that will be used. This will assist in making sure the words are pronounced properly before the students begin creating their movements.
- Syllable Squat is also beneficial to assist with the Spelling Workshop explained in Chapter Six: Plugging in Color.

Chapter 4
Plugging In Patterns

"The brain is, by nature's design, an amazingly subtle and sensitive pattern-detecting apparatus."

—Leslie Hart

Like the intricate web of a garden spider or the never-duplicated design of winter's snowflakes, patterns are a natural part of our world. The brain not only loves the challenge of piecing together the patterns that shape our lives, it actively seeks them out like a hunter in search of prey. Vapid learning environments, devoid of logical patterns, cause the brain to try to make sense out of nonsense, thus creating boredom and, eventually, the chaos of disruption. At best, a more passive learner will comply with empty, meaningless requests and produce the effects of invisible, ghostly learning. But such stagnant learning situations severely stifle any chance of achieving higher levels of thought and learning. As Ellen Langer observes, "Learning the basics in a rote, unthinking manner almost ensures mediocrity" (Langer 24).

From the time a child is in the womb, patterns begin to emerge. The mother notices more movement at particular times of the day, the fetus develops hiccups on a predictable schedule, or the baby reacts to certain sounds each time they occur. These patterns or habits continue through infancy, childhood, and then on into adulthood. The brain takes in sensory input and then processes the information, seeking patterns and connections, in an effort to make sense out of it. "The brain/mind needs and automatically registers the familiar while simultaneously searching for and responding to novel stimuli. In a way, therefore, the brain/mind is both scientist and artist, attempting to discern and understand patterns as they occur and giving expression to unique and creative patterns of its own" (Caine [1997] 105).

Meteorologists use patterns to make their forecasts, farmers use patterns to plant, fertilize, and harvest their crops, and game strategists use patterns to achieve victory. Unfortunately, patterns are not always located or pieced together accurately, and the brain is forced to make sense out of what appears to be nonsense. Caine and Caine (1997) explain that "The brain/mind resists having meaninglessness imposed on it. By meaninglessness, we mean isolated pieces of information unrelated to what makes sense to a particular learner" (105). The more meaningful the learning episode, the deeper the learning will be. "Learners are patterning, or perceiving and creating meaning, all the time in one way or another. We cannot stop them, but we can influence the direction" (Caine and Caine [1994] 89).

We have all experienced situations where we studied for a quiz or a test by simply memorizing information in a rote fashion without paying attention to the important patterns or elaborating on details as the information was encoded. Our goal was merely to make an acceptable score on the test. And we may have been successful in this limited goal—that is, we retrieved the information for the test, but afterward, due to transience, it was lost forever, sucked into some parallel universe where most rote learning eventually ends up. The less meaningful the learning episode is, the less likely that the information is being encoded in a manner that can block the natural effects of transience (see chapter two).

Memories are more easily formed when we can understand patterns that serve as hooks to connect previously learned concepts to new ideas and content. Otherwise, the new information is simply stored briefly in our short-term memory and then flushed out before having the opportunity to transfer to more long-term-memory systems within the brain.

Students who depend on rote memorization to cram for a test are the ones who beg the teacher to "hurry up" and pass out the tests before they forget everything. Unfortunately, these students have not yet discovered that information is better learned in other ways. "Our task as educators… is to help students find relationships between the somewhat random, often trivial fact-filled experiences of everyday life and the fewer enduring principles that define life—and then to help them create and constantly test the memory networks that solidify those relationships" (Sylvester 103).

Solidifying relationships means looking for patterns. Patterns are found in all disciplines, from music, math, art, and science to history, sports and physical education, and language arts. Showing students how to find patterns within and between subjects may prove to be an academic eye-opener for teachers and students alike.

Once we have discovered a pattern, we can more easily retrieve memories associated with the pattern, with only a fraction of the information available. For example, one can simply clap the rhythm of "Happy Birthday" and most people will quickly be able to name the tune. The brain detects the familiar pattern, quickly assimilates other important details about the song, and within seconds can name the song, sing the tune, and recall the last birthday party attended. If we didn't know the pattern, the clapping would appear to be only a random set of sounds with no function or purpose. Sadly, the information many students are exposed to in our classrooms appears to them to be just such random bits of trivia. As teachers, it's our job to guide them to find the patterns, the building blocks of memory and true learning.

Another area of instruction enhanced by observing patterns is the area of student errors. Rather than simply counting errors right or wrong, we need to explore the patterns found within both what students understand and what they do not understand. As a reading teacher sits next to a student who is struggling through the labyrinth of language, he or she, if focusing on patterns of error, will know immediately what help will move the reader forward. If the student stumbles and has difficulty reading words with "ough" and "ould" patterns, then the teacher knows that he or she needs focused instruction on decoding words with these specific patterns. Patterns point to the problem as well as to possible solutions.

Where teachers are willing and able to spend the time to find patterns in students' errors, they can more easily facilitate their students' instructional needs. The lessons presented in such classrooms are student-centered rather than simply following a prescribed scope and sequence derived from textbook chapters or curriculum guides. Increased pressure for higher educational standards is placing greater emphasis on the written, taught, and tested curriculum. This quest for high standards is, of course, valid and noble. However, prescribed calendars of content do not take into consideration the patterns of need for individual students. It is an academic tragedy if a static curriculum wins out at the expense of dynamic learning. Everyone wins if the patterns of errors and the patterns of success are observed with equal vigor.

Last Word

Rationale:

Engaging students in dialogue about language and language exploration is important for vocabulary development.

Objective(s):

Students will explore various language patterns in a fast-paced game that utilizes prior knowledge while also exposing them to new words.

Materials:

Pattern dice (purchased or created)
Index cards (or other paper source)
Timer (one or two minutes)
Pens, pencils, or markers

Presentation Guidelines:

- As always, it is important to model the procedures and process for Last Word as a class before moving students into smaller groups.
- Before beginning the activity, create the pattern dice.

  Option 1: Most teacher stores carry small blank cubes that can be used to create the pattern dice. Word pattern stickers can also be purchased to place on the cubes.

  Option 2: Purchase blank cubes from a craft section of a store and use permanent markers or printed labels to add patterns to the cube.

- Once you have created the dice, model the basic procedures with the class. The game should be modeled orally first.

  1. Roll the dice
  2. If the pattern rolled is *Br*, ask students to turn to a neighbor and take turns saying words that begin with *Br*.

A couple of rules to note:
- No proper nouns
- No words can be repeated
- Variations of words can be used (*walk* and *walking* can both be used)
- No foreign words unless they appear in the English dictionary

3. During the oral round, the last student to successfully provide a *Br* word wins the game. They had the Last Word. The next student must respond with a new word within 10 seconds for the game to continue.

- Once students have played the game orally, they are ready to explore the written version. Having the words written offers additional benefits for spelling, word walls, word sorts, diagnosing strengths and areas of concern such as word knowledge, and so forth.

- The written version requires that the students have index cards or another paper source on which to write their words. Provide each group/table with a stack of index cards. The procedure is similar to the oral version.

1. Roll the die.
2. One student will turn the timer over and the game begins.
3. Students will quickly write one word, in large letters, on each index card. Care should be taken that other students cannot see the words that a student is writing. This stage of the game is solo. I remind the students that they cannot get the Last Word if they share all of their words with others. I also remind them that the more unusual the word is that they write down, the better chance that they will win because someone else will not play their word first.
4. Students must put their pen or pencil down once the time indicated on the timer has elapsed. The words written on the cards now serve as the playing deck for the game.
5. To begin the round, one player will say the word on one of his or her cards as it is turned face up on the center of the table. It is a good strategy to play easier words first. If a word is played that is on another student's card, the duplicate card must be discarded.
6. Students say and play their words, going around in a circle, until one player gets the Last Word by playing the last card. Having the most cards before the game starts does not guarantee a winning hand. Often some of the words are played by other players and must be discarded before they can be used.
7. Smaller groups work well for Last Word because then students are not sitting out too long after running out of cards. Two or three students make a group.

Evaluation/Variations:

- The actual cards that the students create serve as the best evaluation. A certain amount of points can be awarded per card. Example: ten points per card, five points per card, etc., depending on the grade and level of the students.
- Many wonderful variations can be applied to Last Word. Again, the level and grade of the students drive the complexity. The following is a sampling of possible permutations:

  -challenge students to make all words more than one syllable

  -ask for all words to contain a prefix and/or a suffix

  -request that all words relate to a particular content area (science, social studies, math, music, art, sports, etc.)

  -ask that all words be a particular part of speech

- Once students have completed the Last Word game, ask students to take all of the words from their group and sort the words using patterns that they discover (number of syllables, parts of speech, living/nonliving, function, prefixes, suffixes, long I sound, etc.)

Concept Attainment

Rationale:

The best evidence that students truly understand a concept is their ability to express both examples and nonexamples of that concept. Knowing what matches a pattern is important, but knowing what does not match the pattern is important as well. Using the strategy of Concept Attainment is a wonderful way for students to explore patterns of language and to become aware of the importance of those patterns for determining the spelling of words, meanings of words, and the function of words in the English language. "The brain is not a rule applier but a pattern detector" (Cunningham 183). By exploring patterns, in addition to rules, students have a better sense of the various uses of words in the English language.

Objective:

Various language patterns will be explored using the Concept Attainment strategy. Students will then find at least three patterns used in their own writing. Advanced students will be able to use the Concept Attainment strategy and share the patterns located with the class in a metacognitive fashion.

Materials:

Master transparency for Concept Attainment or chart paper

Presentation Guidelines:

- Choose a pattern that you want to explore with the class. There are hundreds, of course, from which to choose. A problem area or a topic you wish to explore as a mini-lesson will be a good choice.
- For the sake of a model, I will use homophones. The concept is never disclosed, in advance, to the students. The importance of Concept Attainment is that the students discover the pattern of the concept by using provided examples and nonexamples. (See Master for Concept Attainment.)
- Using the provided master or a simple T-chart, begin the discussion by saying something along the lines of:

"We are going to explore a language concept today. Rather than telling you what the concept is, I want to see if you can use patterns to discover this common concept. I will provide both examples and nonexamples. The brain loves patterns and will soon start trying to fill in missing pieces. See if you can eventually add more examples and nonexamples and determine the pattern I have in mind. The first example is *there*. A nonexample is *table*."

- Write the examples and nonexamples in the appropriate place as you proceed with the lesson.

  Another example is *rain*. A nonexample is *toadstool*.

- Until two or three examples and nonexamples are provided, there is no way students can use their knowledge of word patterns to discover the concept. I often have students shout out answers after I have given only one example. Be sure to share that this is not using patterns to glean the concept. Our goal is not to guess but to use what we know about words and language.

  Another example is *too*. A nonexample is *rabbit*.

- Careful guidance is a must for this strategy. Often students will begin to determine patterns, both accurate and inaccurate. If a pattern is suggested that matches what you have provided but is not the concept you are moving toward, offer another example and nonexample, making sure the nonexample includes the incorrect pattern the student suggested.

  For example, a student may suggest, based on the words offered so far, that the concept is one-syllable words. This is true (so far) but not the concept I am trying to get.

  I would then say:

  "I like your thinking, but let me give you another example and another nonexample."

  Another example would be *reign*. A nonexample would be *pool*.

  My nonexample, being a one-syllable word, removes that concept as a possibility.

- Rather than ask students to tell you the concept once they think they know what it is, ask them to provide an additional example and nonexample.

  Student M: "I think I know."

  Teacher: "Can you give me an another example of the concept for our chart?"

  Student M: "An example would be *except*."

Teacher:	"Yes, good. Do you have a nonexample?"
Student M:	"Yes, *electricity* would be a nonexample."

- Continue accepting answers from students until it appears most of them know the concept. Then ask the students to name the concept and provide characteristics of the concept.

Teacher:	"It seems that you all have solved the mystery of this pattern. Does anyone know what concept matches the example column of our chart?"
Student Y:	"They are all homophones."
Teacher:	"You are correct. What are the characteristics, then, of homophones that allowed us to find the pattern?"
Student X:	"They are words that sound alike but are spelled differently and have a different meaning."
Teacher:	"What else?"
Student M:	"Some people confuse them and use the wrong version."
Teacher:	"Great. So we know these words require extra effort when we edit to make sure the correct word is being used."

- This method of exploring a concept requires a great deal of attention and focus, thereby increasing the attention given to the concept's attributes. Worksheets rarely, if ever, explore the nonexamples and thus can make it appear that students understand a concept when in reality they do not.

Evaluation/Variations:

- True evaluation for this activity comes from being able to determine whether students can find examples and nonexamples of patterns.
- Younger students may only be able to complete the oral version of Concept Attainment with the teacher. That alone is incredibly beneficial and should not be discounted due to the advanced levels of critical thinking required.
- Older or more advanced students will be able to follow the process of concept attainment with patterns used in their own writing.
  - Ask students to get out a recently completed composition. This is ideal if they're keeping portfolios. Otherwise, have students do this extension of Concept Attainment after completing their next composition. Challenge students to find one or two word patterns used in the composition. At least three or four words will be needed for other students to determine the pattern. (See Exploring Word Patterns handout on page 64)
  - If time permits, or as a possible assessment, students can then present their concept to the class to allow other students the opportunity to discover the pattern.
  - Again, the depth of exploration forces students to become more metacognitive about the word and language patterns used in their own writing and in the writing of others. These patterns often impact the writer's style, tone, and voice.
  - The discovery and discussion is crucial for deepening students' understanding of language.

Concept Attainment

Examples	Nonexamples

Concept:

Characteristics of Concept:

Exploring Language Patterns

Name: _____

Date: _____

Composition or Published Text Explored: _____

I noticed the following concept/pattern in the writing/text: _____

Examples as evidence:

_____

_____

_____

_____

I noticed the following concept/pattern in the writing/text: _____

Examples as evidence:

_____

_____

_____

_____

I noticed the following concept/pattern in the writing/text: _____

Examples as evidence:

_____

_____

_____

_____

Pattern Sacks

Rationale:

As complex as the English language may be, one reassuring fact is that it follows patterns. Spelling, grammar, sentence structure, vocabulary words, etc., all follow patterns. Students need to observe the patterns rather than trying to memorize the rules. Trying to learn and remember all the rules is a frustrating and nearly impossible task for those who are not constantly immersed in language at the deepest levels. Even a master physician cannot possibly retrieve all of the facts, theories, and disease profiles he or she learned in medical school when making a diagnosis. Rather, the physician relies on the patterns he or she has seen develop over time. Likewise, users of language rely on the occurrence and reoccurrence of patterns in words. "Information about a word is gained from its spelling (orthography), its pronunciation (phonology), it meaning (semantics), and the contexts in which the word occurs. The brain processes these sources of information in parallel, or simultaneously. The brain functions in word recognition, as it does in all other areas, as a pattern detector" (Cunningham 184).

Objective:

Students will explore various patterns of language through this interactive sorting activity.

Materials:

Sacks (e.g. plain paper lunch bags or colored gift bags)
Magazines
Scissors
Glue sticks
String (if using the ceiling to publish)
Index cards

Presentation Guidelines:

- Divide students into groups of two or three.
- Each group will get a sack, an index card, scissors, and a few magazines (at least one per person).
- Brainstorm, with students, possible word patterns: adjectives, verbs, nouns, long I sound, two syllable words, proper nouns, similes, and so forth.
- Ask students to look through the magazines and find words or phrases that follow any language or word pattern they discover. At least 10 words must be located for the pattern to be shared. All of the words the group cuts out should match one pattern that the group agrees on. Encourage students to make the pattern as challenging as possible. Give students 10 to 15 minutes to find their words or phrases.

- Students will write on the index card what the pattern is for their words, and they will write their names on the same side of the card.
- The index card should be placed, facedown, inside the bag (where the pattern will not show). One small dab of glue should be used to keep the card from falling out when the bag is turned upside down.
- All of the collected pattern words or phrases will then be placed in the sack.
- Either the same day or another day, the sacks will be redistributed so that the groups do not get their own sack. Each group will be given another index card. The group will then analyze the words from the sack they have been given and, through discussion, determine the pattern.
- The group should write what they think the pattern is on the new index card and should write each group member's name on the card as well. The card at the bottom of the sack will be removed to verify that the creating group and the analyzing group had the same pattern in mind.
- The analyzing group will then find 10 more words from their magazines that match the pattern they have just explored. Both cards are lightly glued to the bottom of the sack.
- The sacks can be exchanged as many times as desired. At the end of the exchange cycle (one day, two days, a week, etc), the initial index card that names the pattern and the words are glued down to the outside of the sack. Encourage students to use the most unique and colorful words first as some of the words may not fit, depending on how many times the sack was exchanged.
- The sacks should then be published, either by hanging them from the ceiling or some other creative form of display

Long A pattern sack.

Evaluation/Variations:

- The pattern sacks can be evaluated numerous ways. After the initial searching and cutting, a grade can be given if students discovered a logical pattern and located the 10 words to illustrate the pattern.
- And/or a grade can be given after the exchange if the group discovered the correct pattern and accurately added 10 additional words.
- And/or have students select or be assigned one of the patterns once the sacks are published, and challenge students to find words matching the pattern from their own writings.

Word Stamps

Rationale:

Rehearsal of known words is important. Likewise, having an awareness of the relationship between words helps strengthen memory traces. Word Stamps allows students to make associations and then connections with words generated through the activity. The learning and rehearsal of language that this activity offers are powerful. Each student will benefit from the exploration and discussion involved, no matter at what age or instructional level.

Objective:

Students will make word connections with stamped images. The generated word connections will then be sorted into meaningful categories. The selecting, sorting, and synthesizing process is where the rehearsal and learning of words occur.

Materials:

Large piece of square paper (12x12 works well)
A collection of rubber stamps (see sample stamp collection on page 72); four stamps will work, but a larger variety is recommended
Dictionary and thesaurus

Presentation Guidelines:

- Two options are available for beginning Word Stamps.
    1. Pre-stamp the four corners of each 12x12 piece of paper with four different stamps (this is a good option for the first time you use this strategy).
    2. Allow students (two students for each sheet of paper) to select four stamps out of your collection and carefully stamp the four corners of the paper. Initially students should not be told what the stamped images are going to be used for.
- Discuss with students the importance of constantly reviewing and rehearsing words they know and the relationships between those words. Students should also make mental notes and observations about words they do not know. This dialogue about words and language is ongoing and should occur, at some level, on a daily basis.
- Because we want students to be exposed to additional words, it is good to have them work in pairs for this activity.

- Ask students, as you model, to fold the large paper in half, corner to corner.

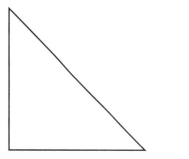 

- Students should then fold the paper in half again from the other side. The creases will create four triangles.

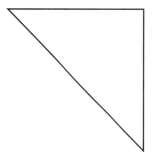 

- Now ask students to fold each of the four corners into the center of the paper as if they are making a pinwheel.

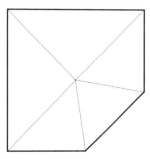

- Once the paper is unfolded, it will be creased as follows:

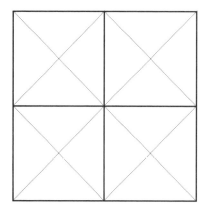

- Showing your premade example (see samples on page 70), model how students will write down words that come to mind from each of the stamped images. Students will write the words in each corner around the corresponding stamped image. Students do not have to explore one corner at a time. They can write down words in a random fashion. Often students will be working on one corner and suddenly think of a word for a different corner.

- The words written down only need to be associated in some way to the stamped image. The relationship does not have to be direct. I encourage students to try to brainstorm a minimum of five words per corner. Remind students that they do not have to accurately spell every word they put down. If they are unsure of the spelling, ask them to circle the word so it can be checked at a later time.

- After students have spent several minutes brainstorming words, I share a strategy for digging deeper for more words by asking students to mentally go through all content areas to specifically focus on content-specific language.

  What geography or history words might be associated with each image? What art words...? What science words...? What physical education or sports words...? What math words...? What music words...?

  Using this method to focus the search for words, I challenge students to add at least four more words to their stamp page.

- As students are finalizing their stamp lists, point out and praise higher-level words and words from other content areas that you note on students' stamp sheets. Often other students will add these words to their own sheets.

- Next students will move to the challenge of finding patterns and connections between the words on their Word Stamp. Show students the four squares in the middle of the page and the four blank triangles discovered by folding the corners back into the center of the page. These areas will be used to sort the words from all four corners into categories.

- It is crucial to brainstorm, with students, possible patterns (categories) that the words can be sorted into. The discussion will depend on the age and level of the students and what they have learned so far about language. The more students know about language, the more categories they will be able to create. It is okay if students only know a few possibilities when they first go through this process. Through sharing, collaboration, and focused, meaningful language study, they will get better and more advanced. (See Possible Pattern Guide on page 71)

- Challenge students to place all of the words on their stamp page into one or more categories. With the help of students, I have provided a Possible Pattern Guide, below, to scaffold students through this process. Blank areas have been intentionally left so that students can add on to the possibilities.

- The process of this activity drives the learning. The exploration is meaningful, fast paced, and diagnostic. The words and categories generated provide a great deal of information about students' knowledge of words and language patterns.
- Give students time to share their Word Stamps. It is good to ask them to share the three most complex words they generated and to share the categories they placed their words into.
- If students had words that did not match any of the categories, ask them to share what unique characteristics these words have that would exclude them from the categories they generated.

Evaluation/Variations:

- A grade can be given based on the number of words generated and/or for the sorting of the words into categories.
- The next time you utilize the Word Stamp activity, allow students to choose the four stamps.
- Use the same stamps six weeks later and see if students can generate more words.
- For extra credit or for an extension, ask students to locate their three most complex words in a meaningful context. Give them a set time period to complete this task.
- Stickers or stamping markers can be used as images to generate words as well. This is a nice variation to employ after the stamps have been used.

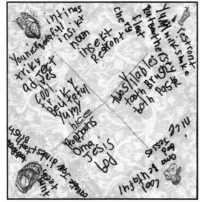

2nd Grade Word Stamp Sample

6th Grade Word Stamp Sample

Possible Pattern Guide

Nouns	Living/ Nonliving	Words with Suffixes	Words related To Life cycles	Words related to Fantasy genre
Proper Nouns	Words That Rhyme	History Words	Slang Terms	Words With Foreign Origin
Verbs	Long I Sound	Words Using blends	Homographs	Words Related To Sports
Compound Words	Homophones	Long E Sound	Words dealing With size	Words dealing With love
Adjectives	Words from Mythology	Words with Double Consonants	Long O Sound	Words about Animals
One syllable Words	Words about Writing	Words that Are negative	Math words	Words Relating To Art
Two syllable Words	Words with Vowels	Words with Prefixes	Color Words	Words Related To Geography
Three Syllable Words	Words that Are Positive	Words Related to School	Four or more Syllables	Science Words

Sample Stamp Collection

			THANK YOU MERCI GRACIA ARIGATO DAN
	DARE TO DREAM		
ROUGH DRAFT			
!			
			UNDER CONSTRUCTION

Vocabulary Unplugged • ©2005 Alana Morris • www.discoverwriting.com

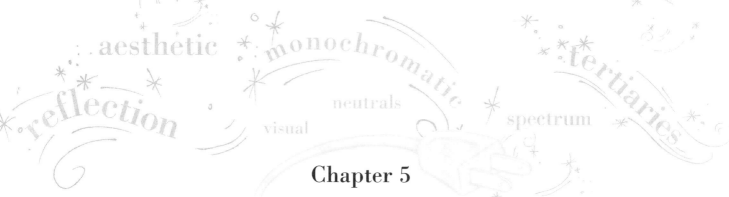

Chapter 5
Plugging In Color

"Color is one of the most powerful tools for enhancing memory and creativity."
–Tony Buzan

When architects changed classroom walls from orange and white to blue, students' blood pressure dropped, and their behavior and learning comprehension increased (Walker 4). Experiments such as this have been studied for years. An increased number of studies are being developed and explored due to the explosion in knowledge and research regarding the brain and learning. Like music, color sends off waves. These waves are essential for the learning environment.

Understanding the psychological and physiological properties of color can benefit teachers in the preparation and delivery of lessons. Like music, color sends off waves, and the quality of these waves is essential to the learning environment. The role color plays in emotional states, memory, and learning in general is important for both teachers and students. Far too many classrooms offer little or no visual stimulation within their walls. Not only are the vapid, bland walls of some classrooms visually unappealing, they may actually be lessening the chances for more solid learning opportunities. Research shows that the use of color can be a simple step that leads to vast improvements across many layers of the learning experience.

Color adds more to our lives than we consciously realize. The colors we choose for our clothing, our home environments, public places, our places of work (if we have a choice here), and our schools affect us greatly, for better and for worse. When one company chose to experiment by painting office walls red, production went up dramatically; however, by the afternoon hours, the employees were arguing and had extreme difficulty getting along with one another (Walker xii).

Red and blue tend to have opposite effects, because red is a "warm" color and blue is a "cool" color. They are on opposite ends of the color spectrum, so it makes sense that they would have opposite psychological effects. When a person with hypertension swims in a blue swimming pool, his or her blood pressure temporarily lowers (Walker xi).

The effects of color on human beings go back thousands of years. Max Luscher explains that the basic dichotomy of light and dark began with early man. "Night brought passivity, quiescence, and a general slowing down of metabolic and glandular activity. Day brought with it the possibility of actions, an increase in the metabolic rate and greater glandular secretion, thus providing him with both energy and incentive" (18). It should not be surprising, then, that dark cool colors would affect us in one way and light warm colors would affect us in another. "Every color sends out either high or low vibrations that create a feeling of warmth or coolness" (Walker 36). In the same way that we can control states of mind with sound waves (music), we can control emotional states with light waves.

Dramatic studies show that the walls of our classrooms are not simply invisible barriers to separate and divide; they are canvases of emotion that affect our students each day. Dr. Morton Walker explains that many chemical changes occur within the brain to cause the various feelings we experience with color. For example, when exposed to red, a person's pituitary gland (an endocrine gland) sends a chemical signal to the adrenal gland and epinephrine (adrenaline) is released (50). Even colorblind people experience this excitatory effect, though they cannot perceive the color red through the retina as most people do. Likewise, bulls are affected by the color red even though they are believed to be colorblind.

A lasting color impression is made within ninety seconds, and this impression accounts for 60 percent of whether a person, place, event, or circumstance is experienced as either positive or negative (70). When blue is in a person's field of vision, for example, it causes the brain to secrete eleven neurotransmitters that have a tranquilizing effect (52). Yellow, on the other hand, is the color that the eye registers the quickest. Massive amounts of yellow tend to increase anxiety and cause tempers to flare. The bottom line is that every color sends out either a low or a high vibration rate that results in a sense of security or uncertainty.

The eye is not the only part of the body to take in the color waves. "The aura, skin response, brain response, and also heartbeat, respiration, blood pressure, seem to be involved with color through electrical impulses" (Birren 81). Birren (1978) explains that even infrared and ultraviolet lights, which are invisible, will cause reflex actions. This further supports the belief that the body reacts to color in multifaceted ways, both with and without the eyes' assistance. Delacroix, the famous Renaissance painter, once remarked, "Colors are the music of the eyes. They combine like notes. Certain color harmonies produce feelings that music itself could not attain" (Huyghe 158).

As teachers, we must be sure that the color music in our classrooms harmonizes with the emotional states that are most conducive to learning. Certainly educators should not go overboard, painting rainbows and color splashes throughout their classrooms. But research has increasingly shown the value of being aware of how our classroom environments look, and how color is used within their walls.

Color My World

Rationale:

The brain loves color, and the brain naturally seeks connections and associations. The use of color in an activity adds depth to the words being explored and increases memory connections. Often students can know the definition of a word or concept but not understand that definition. In this activity, in order to make a connection between the word and a color, students must understand, at a conceptual level, the definition of the word.

Objective(s):

Students will choose words that can be paired with a Crayola crayon. Students must clearly understand the definition of the word to explain the reason the word connects to the color.

Materials:

Box of 96 Crayola crayons
Glue
Dictionary and/or other resources for new words, or a list of unique or specially chosen words (content-based, etc.)
Construction paper
Various books about color (see list on page 94)

Presentation Guidelines:

- Read one of many books about color. I love Ken Nordine's *Color*, created after his 1967 spoken word poetry CD by the same title.
- Explain that color is a wonderful way for the brain to remember new vocabulary words.
- The activity can be completed by selecting a word that matches a color or by selecting a color and finding matching words.
- Model the process by choosing a crayon from the box such as Razzle Dazzle Rose.
- Show the color to students and ask them to think of the color as a person. What personality traits, emotions, and ideas would Razzle Dazzle Rose have? "Serene" and "calm" would probably not come to mind.

Here is a list that a fifth-grade class generated:

Energetic

Obnoxious

Stuck up

Likes to dance

Wears too much makeup

Flirts

Hangs out at the mall

Pretty

Expensive tastes

Bright fingernail polish

- Now students will choose their own colors (you may choose to have students work in pairs).

- They will then brainstorm a list of words and phrases for their color. (It is interesting how many students choose colors much like their own personalities.)

- Students will then use their list and other resources for words and find a noun, a verb, and an adjective that match the color's characteristics that they brainstormed. Each of the three words must be a challenging word.

- Of course, challenging is always relative, so I suggest to students that the word should be one that most students would not know or would not use often. For example, from the Razzle Dazzle Rose brainstorm, *obnoxious* would be preferred over *pretty*.

- The brainstormed list of traits generally will not be sufficient. Students will have to dig into the dictionary and other sources to find what they feel are the perfect words.

- Using the color sketch pad (student handout on page 78), students will include the word, part of speech, and how the word is connected to the color. The challenge here is that the definition of the word must be woven into the explanation.

- The assignment can stop at the color sketch pad; however, if time permits, taking the activity to the publishing stage is great for displaying the words and for providing further lessons in revision and/or editing.

- For publishing, students will creatively display the three words and responses, including the actual crayon in some fashion.

Evaluation/Variations:

- If there is a list of words students must learn for a particular content class or reading selection, then take the activity in the opposite direction of that modeled earlier. Begin with the word and then ask students to find the perfect color that matches the word and tell why. The definition, again, should be woven into the explanation.

- Depending on the total objectives covered and the time spent on the activity, a rubric should be used to assess and score the assignment. Separate grades might be given for the brainstorming, the sketch pad draft, and then the final published piece. It is important that the rubric for scoring reflect the actual objectives taught and expected.

- If you own or have access to a Crayola maker, which came out in the fall of 2002, it is wonderful to assist students in making crayons and then to have them give the colors unique names (I have students use an adjective in their color name).

- Peel the labels off the colors and have students create unique names, again making sure to use a challenging adjective. You can cut mailing labels that students can then design for their crayon with its new name.

- Crayola has a wonderful website worth exploring. It is www.crayola.com. Much information about each color can be researched via the site.

Students' Favorite Crayola Crayon Colors for Connections

Tickle Me Pink	Cyber Grape	Forest Green	Tropical Rain Forest	Dandelion	Bitter Sweet
Blizzard Blue	Razzmatazz	Vivid Tangerine	Denim	Shamrock	Navy Blue
Granny Smith Apple	Robin's Egg Blue	Magic Mint	Purple Pizzazz	Shocking Pink	Hot Magenta
Macaroni and Cheese	Outrageous Orange	Timberwolf	Wisteria	Fuchsia	Wild Strawberry
Atomic Tangerine	Carnation Pink	Midnight Blue	Mulberry	Copper	Mauvelous
Purple Mountain's Majesty	Laser Lemon	Chestnut	Tumbleweed	Sea green	Melon

Color Sketch Pad

Word (noun):

Definition:

Color:

Part of speech:

Explain how the word is connected to the color. Be sure to fully develop your ideas.

Word (verb):

Definition:

Color:

Part of speech:

Explain how the word is connected to the color. Be sure to fully develop your ideas.

Word (adjective):

Definition:

Color:

Part of speech:

Explain how the word is connected to the color. Be sure to fully develop your ideas.

Spelling Workshop

Rationale:

Color energizes memory. We learn thousands of words in our lives without the aid of color; however, students are often asked to learn words out of a natural context, are asked to learn numerous words at a time, or have a neurological difference that traditional word study does not accommodate. Since it can help to better remember and spell newly acquired words, color is a tool that even the most advanced connoisseur of words would do well to explore. Knowing the definitions of words without being able to accurately spell them will hinder the students' efforts to use the words in their writing. Simply copying words twenty times is not beneficial for most students.

Objective:

Students will explore four different techniques, utilizing patterns and color to enhance their ability to spell words they have learned through a variety of strategies.

Materials:

Markers, colors, gel pens, colored pencils, etc.
Workshop guide papers
List of words
Letter for parents (optional)

Presentation Guidelines:

- Share with students that if they use the techniques you are going to share with them, their spelling will improve greatly.

- The brain loves color and the brain loves patterns. Both are used in the Spelling Workshop.

- The first adventure for the Spelling Workshop is to divide the words into syllables. The key is to use a different color for each syllable. One-syllable words will remain one color. No black or blue ink or pencils should be used for this part of the workshop. The vivid colors used are crucial for enhancing memory.

    Example: Exaggerate   Ex   ag   ger   ate

Each of the four syllables will be in a different color.

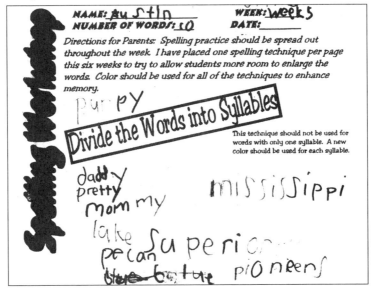

- The second adventure in the spelling workshop is to exaggerate the trouble spot. Again, color is important. Wherever the trouble area is, it should be exaggerated in size and with color.

    Example: If *receive* is misspelled *recieve*, it will become   re**CEI**ve

- Make students aware that they should pay close attention as they complete the tasks. If each part of the workshop is completed mindlessly, there will be little success. The brain must be tuned in.

- The third workshop adventure requiring color is to explore patterns and/or memory connections. Students should try to locate a common pattern in the misspelled words. I encourage looking for word or letter patterns first before moving to patterns in meaning. An example of a meaning-based pattern would be if a student misspelled Wednesday, he or she would then write Sunday and Saturday as a possible pattern. The age and developmental level of the student will determine how complex a pattern the student will be able to locate independently.

    Example of a sound pattern: Receive   Pattern: ei following c
                         per**cei**ve, de**cei**ve, re**cei**pt

The portion of the words that drive the pattern should be enhanced in size and color. Students should try to find at least three additional words that match the pattern. The color used in each of these tasks allows the brain to form stronger memory connections between the word patterns and the spellings.

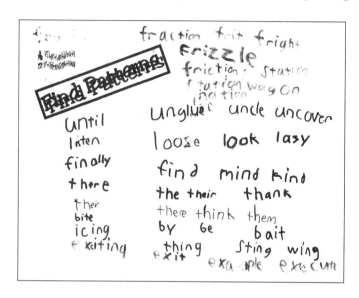

If patterns cannot be located, or in addition to locating patterns, students are asked to find meaningful connections or memory aids.

Example: Station**a**ry versus station**e**ry

These are homophones that can be difficult to tell apart since only one letter differentiates them. A memory aid would be to connect the different letter to its meaning as follows:

Station**e**ry- The **e** in this word connects to the **e** in l**e**tter, meaning paper on which letters are written.

Station**a**ry- The **a** in this word is connected to the **a** in stand, meaning to st**a**nd stationary.

• The final workshop adventure asks students to find words within words. Students will try to find at least three smaller words within each word from their lists. I ask that they first try to find actual words in sequence. Only after those possibilities have been exhausted should they try to locate words that can be created from the scrambled letters.

Example: *exaggerate*   Words in sequence: ex, ate, rat, rate, at, era

                        Words from scrambled letters: egg, axe, gate, grate, etc.

Both are beneficial for assisting the memory systems. Again, ask students to write the words found within the words in color.

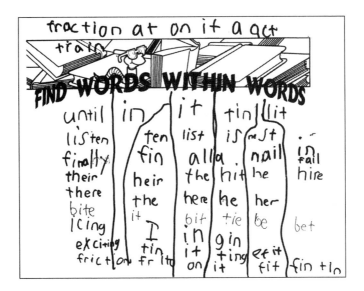

Evaluation/Variation:

- Teachers may choose to evaluate the Spelling Workshop in a variety of ways.
- I use the workshop as homework. Each night the students complete a different workshop adventure (task). The assessment then follows. The students actually complete the workshop using words that have been misspelled in their own writings or vocabulary words recently studied. Again, knowing the spelling of new words studied will build confidence for actually using the words in writing.
- Each of the sheets for the Spelling Workshop has been included. These may be altered to meet the needs of your students.

Name: _____

Date: _____

Directions for Workshop: Spelling practice should be spread out throughout the week. I have given one spelling study technique per page to allow students plenty of room to enlarge the words. Each evening, one technique will be completed. Color should be used for all of the techniques to enhance memory.

Adventure One: Divide each of your spelling words into syllables. Each syllable should be written in a new color. One-syllable words will remain one color.

Spelling Workshop: Adventure One
Divide the Words into Syllables

Name: _____

Date: _____

Adventure Two: Exaggerate the trouble spot by enhancing the size and color of the problem area.

Spelling Workshop: Adventure Two

Exaggerate the trouble spot

Name: _____

Date: _____

Adventure Three: Locate Patterns and/or Memory Connections for the words from your list. Try to find at least three sound or spelling patterns that match your word(s) and enhance the pattern with color. Clearly write out the explanation for any memory connections you make.

Spelling Workshop: Adventure Three
Patterns and/or Memory Connections

Name: _____

Date: _____

Adventure Four: Find words within the words from your list. Try to locate at least three words that are within the word and in the same order. Write each word in a new color.

Example: delicate cat, at, ate

Once you have found words in the same order, you can try to find words with the scrambled letters from your word. Write each word in a new color.

Example: delicate tile, lid, late

Scavenger Hunt

Rationale:

Once students learn various attributes and aspects of words, it is important that they get opportunities to explore the characteristics of language that they have learned. Often students learn a word, a rule, or a pattern but never get the opportunity to move quickly enough to some type of application or exploration. The Scavenger Hunt allows students to dig and explore for the words and patterns they have learned. This activity provides multiple contexts and strengthens the memory and understanding of the words.

Objective(s):

Students will hunt for various word patterns and rules, using colored highlighting tape. This gamelike hunt provides motive, challenge, and purpose, which enhance the learning experience.

Materials:

Highlighting strips
Highlighting tape can be purchased, but it is often expensive. I prefer using Hotcolor brand neon book covers. These come in five neon colors that can be cut into approximately 1" x .5" small strips. The students are then able to peel the backing off and place the strips (word darts) directly onto the text being used for the hunt. (Note: Highlighters can also be used; however, the peeling of the strips actually helps slow down the cognitive process. Often students mark texts too quickly and without thinking when using highlighters.)
Text(s) for hunting: novels, trade books, song lyrics, newspapers, magazines, textbooks, students' own writing. Any text or multiple texts can be used for the Scavenger Hunt. This is a strategy that utilizes multiple concepts and learning opportunities at one time. Scavenger Hunt Direction Sheet for each team (I laminate these so they can be used multiple times).

Presentation Guidelines:

- The procedure for the Scavenger Hunt is simple. The benefits, however, are complex and well worth the advance preparation.
- Before the actual hunt, decide what previously learned word patterns you would like your students to explore. These words or patterns should be placed on a Scavenger Hunt Direction Page.
  *See sample Scavenger Hunt Directions A, B, and C, on pages 89-91.

- Likewise, decide what type of text(s) will be used for the hunt. Notice that the three sample Scavenger Hunts use different formats to show a few of the many possibilities.
- Gather the needed materials for the hunt: text(s), highlighting strips, Scavenger Hunt Direction Sheets (pages 89-91).
- Place the students into pairs or groups of no more than three students.
- Set a workable time limit for the search. Searches can be repeated with less time at a later date because students will already know the procedures. The time provided will depend on the grade and level of the students.
- The format of the Scavenger Hunt does not require that all students complete the entire list of words being hunted. The learning is driven by the process (20 minutes is a good amount of time for most students).
- Once each group has the direction sheet, the search is on.
- Give each student several highlighting strips. I have found that this helps to make sure that all students are involved with the search rather than just one.
- Remind students that they must not split up to find the patterns. Only one source can be explored at a time by the team. Again, this requires the team to work together to find the patterns. Much learning takes place in the discussion and collaboration during the search.
- You can decide if you want to have an actual winning team or give all teams a chance to win within the time allotted. The latter keeps all students engaged for the duration of the activity.
- After the Scavenger Hunt has ended, ask each team to share some of the words they found. I ask teams to share words they believe no other team will have found. The sharing time is crucial. The learning is in the discussion.

Evaluation/Variations:

- Students can hunt solo as an assessment once they are familiar with the process.
- The Scavenger Hunt itself is easy to assess. For each pattern found, the students get ten points. If your direction sheet has fewer or more patterns to locate, the point scale would change accordingly.
- The Scavenger Hunt is wonderful to use for other language concepts as well: parts of speech, sentence structure patterns, dialogue patterns, types/functions of paragraphs, and so forth.

Scavenger Hunt Directions A

You and your partner(s) will carefully explore the books, newspapers, and magazines for the language patterns listed below. Use your colored word darts to mark the words you find. Be prepared to share what you find. Collect your evidence as you go. Make sure you know the definition of all words discovered and can show the source where it was found.

Find two words that are two syllables and have a long vowel sound.

_____   _____

Find one word that is four syllables.

_____

Locate two compound words.

_____   _____

Find a word that is an antonym for old.

_____

Find two positive and two negative words.

_____   _____   _____   _____

Scavenger Hunt Directions B

You and your partner(s) will carefully explore the books, newspapers, and magazines for the language patterns listed below. Use your colored word darts to mark the words you find. Be prepared to share what you find. Collect your evidence as you go. Make sure you know the definition of all words discovered and can show the source where each one was found.

Find a word that is <u>two syllables</u> and rhymes with <u>hand</u>.

_____

Find <u>one</u> word that is <u>three syllables</u>.

_____

Locate a <u>proper noun</u> containing the <u>long A (a)</u> sound.

_____

Find a word that is a <u>synonym</u> for <u>good</u>.

_____

Find <u>two</u> words that have <u>double consonants</u>.

_____   _____

Locate two words that each contain a suffix that makes the words adjectives.

_____   _____

Scavenger Hunt Directions C

You and your partner(s) will carefully explore books, newspapers, and magazines for the language patterns listed below. Use your colored word darts to mark the words you find. Be prepared to share what you find. Collect your evidence as you go. Make sure you know the definition of all words discovered and can show the source where each one was found.

Locate any form of figurative language (simile, metaphor, hyperbole, idiom, etc.)

_____

Find two words containing the same prefix.

_____   _____

Find two nouns that are three syllables.

_____   _____

Track down a word that comes from another country.

_____

Find <u>two words</u> that are less than 100 years old. Be able to explain where and/or how the words originated.

_____   _____

Locate <u>two words</u> that relate to <u>mathematics</u>.

_____   _____

Word Balloons

Rationale:

Current brain research suggests that color, the environment, and peripherals in the classroom are important to learning. Much of what we learn is filtered through this form of exposure to information. This activity uses the environment, color, and graphics to aid students in remembering words. All students will benefit from this environmental experience with our language, especially if they are visual learners. Students who are kinesthetic learners will greatly enjoy the hands-on creation of the 3-D visual that is part of the assignment. The process of creating the visual and the color used enhance memory of the word(s) explored.

Objective(s):

Students will use clear, large balloons to create a visual representation of a word or concept.

Materials:

Clear balloons (may be purchased in bulk at a craft store); larger balloons can be special-ordered via the Internet from a balloon wholesaler
Permanent markers
Paper and materials needed for the visual display (sharp objects or objects with edges will create obvious problems)

Presentation Guidelines:

- Students will be assigned or will select one spelling or vocabulary word from a teacher-generated list. These can include words from content areas: my second graders, when studying weather, each created a weather condition for their visual display (fog, hurricane, thunderstorm, etc.). Another example would be a math class studying geometric shapes. The structure can be seen on the inside of the balloon while the word can be designed with more images on the outside.
- Students will create objects or pictures that visually represent their word.
- These objects are carefully placed within the balloon. The balloon can be stretched; however, the objects cannot be too large or they will not go inside the balloon. Because the balloons are clear, the objects can be clearly seen inside. **Again, sharp objects or edges will puncture the balloon.**

Vocabulary Unplugged • ©2005 Alana Morris • www.discoverwriting.com

- Students or teachers (depending on the age) should be careful not to inflate the balloons too much, as they expand with heat and may pop overnight-especially if you live in a warm climate where the air conditioning is turned off in the evening. This created a great science lesson for my classes one year (not intentionally, of course!).

- Making sure the tie of the balloon is facing up (for publishing reasons), students will write the word on the outside of the balloon using the colored permanent marker(s). Some students choose to write the word in a way that also represents its meaning. However, the words should still be easy to read.

- After the balloons are complete, a large paper clip should be opened out to serve as a hook. The balloons are then hung from the ceiling. The words and the graphic connections can then be shared. Again, this becomes a form of Word Wall to which students will definitely pay attention.

- The visual effect offers stimulation and exposes the students to many new words in a multimodal fashion. It can't help but "lighten up" the students' attitude about vocabulary study.

Evaluation/Variations:

- Using a rubric is the best way to assess the word balloons.
- Rather than simply using random vocabulary words, you can explore various parts of speech such as adjectives, verbs, collective nouns, etc.
- Content words can be explored: music, science, geography, math, etc.

Collection of Color Books

Carle, Eric. 1998. *Hello, Red Fox*. New York, New York: Simon and Schuster Books.

Collins, Pat Lowery. 1992. *I am an Artist*. Brookfield, Connecticut: The Millbrook Press.

Color. 1996. New York: Scholastic.

Friend, Catherine. 1994. *My Head is Full of Colors*. New York, New York: Hyperion Books.

Gifaldi, David. 1993. *The Boy Who Spoke Colors*. Boston, Massachusetts: Houghton Mifflin Company.

Godwin, Patricia. 1993. *I Feel Orange Today*. New York, New York: Annick Press.

Heller, Ruth. 1995. *Color*. New York, New York: Putnam and Grosset.

Hindley, Judy. 1998. *A Song of Colors*. Cambridge, Massachusetts: Candlewick Press.

Hubbard, Patricia. 1996. *My Crayons Talk*. New York, New York: Henry Holt and Company.

Joosse, Barbara. 1996. *I Love You the Purplest*. San Francisco, California: Chronicle Books.

Nordine, Ken. 2000. *Colors*. San Diego, California: Harcourt.

Seuss, Dr. 1996. *My Many Colored Days*. New York, New York: Alfred A. Knopf.

Shalom, Vivienne. 1995. *The Color of Things*. New York, New York: Rizzoli.

Whitman, Candace. 1998. *Bring on the Blue*. New York, New York: Abbeville Kids.

Whitman, Candace. 1998. *Ready for Red*. New York, New York: Abbeville Kids.

Whitmen, Candace. 1998. *Yellow and You*. New York, New York: Abbeville Kids.

Wilson. April. 1999. *Magpie Magic*. New York, New York: Dial Books.

Chapter 6
Plugging In Music and Sound

"Sound touches us with an eloquent and universal language that speaks to our very cells."

–Thomas Kenyon

"M-I-crooked letter-crooked letter-I-crooked letter-crooked letter-I-hump back-hump back-I." This rhythmic chant has helped young people recall the spelling of Mississippi for years. The familiar alphabet song uses rhythm and melody in the same manner to help the very youngest children learn their letters. As educators, our knowledge of how music and sound enhance learning can help orchestrate states of learning within our classrooms with the same fine precision as the conductor of the New York Philharmonic. Each downbeat, each individual musician, and each careful calculation of tempo adds to the success of the concert. The score (blueprint) of a musical composition is layered and complex, but a well-trained conductor knows what is going on at every moment and how each of the parts harmonizes or creates dissonance with the others. Hence, when someone is out of tune, a rhythm is off, or the balance doesn't seem quite right, the conductor can make the appropriate changes immediately through signals and gestures the musicians recognize. Through the use of music, teachers can also change the pacing, tone, and balance of their learning environments. This does not mean simply *playing* music, but rather using music effectively to enhance learning.

As with language, students' exposure to music and sound begins even before birth, in the mother's womb. The sound of the mother's voice and the steady rhythmic beat of her heart wrap the child in a daily pulsating blanket of security. These rhythms continue to offer feelings of safety and comfort throughout a child's life, and the effects remain long afterward, into adulthood.

The calming impact of sound has been observed for centuries. Needing no research to back up their instinctive knowledge of the power of song, mothers rock their children and sing lullabies to get them to sleep. Sue Chapman, M.D., conducted a study in a New York City Hospital with premature infants where one group was continuously exposed to the music of Brahms while a control group heard no music. The "Brahms babies" had fewer complications, gained weight faster, and were released an average of a week earlier than the control group (Kenyon 181). These results were no coincidence; the impact of music goes well beyond the walls of nurseries.

Robert MacNeil, former cohost of *The MacNeil-Lehrer Report* and narrator of the PBS series *The Story of English*, has spent his life exploring words and language. In his incredible memoir, *WordStruck*, he elaborates on the connection between music and words.

> It must be with words as it is with music. Music heard early in life lays down a rich bed of memories against which you evaluate and absorb music encountered later. Each layer adds to the richness of your musical experience; it ingrains expectations that will govern your taste for future music and perhaps change your feelings about music you already know. Certain harmonic patterns embed themselves in your consciousness and create yearnings for repetition, so that you can relive that pleasurable disturbance of the soul. Gradually, your head becomes an unimaginable large jukebox, with instantaneous recall and cross-referencing, far more sophisticated than anything man-made.
> (23–24)

Though typically not considered a language itself, music has deep and natural connections with both written and spoken language. These connections include such aspects as tone, audience, voice, rhythm, style, tempo, and fluency. What distinguishes the two is that "Music has no words, no syllables, no nouns or verbs, and no plurals or tenses; it has no way to name people, objects or actions, no way to count, no way to say whether something is true or false, and no way to ask questions or give instructions" (Jackendoff 165). However, by connecting music with reading and writing, we make abstract concepts, such as voice, inference, and tone more accessible.

Ronald Kotulak, author of *Inside the Brain*, states that "Music... besides being enjoyable, appears to be able to increase brain power, possibly by exercising the same circuits employed in memory formation" (141). This is not a novel concept born out of modern brain research. *Rhapsodes*, in the days of Homer and earlier, were professional reciters who employed the power of song to recall and recount long epic stories to spellbound listeners. Anthony Storr, in *Music and the Mind*, expands, with evidence, what we have known instinctively for hundreds of years:

> The mnemonic power of music is still evident in modern culture. Many of us remember the words of songs and poems more accurately than we can remember prose. That music facilitates memory has been confirmed by the study of mentally retarded children who can recall more material after it is given to them in a song than after it is read to them as a story. (21)

The "ability to manipulate sounds" is referred to as phonological or *phonemic awareness* (Cunningham 10). It is a child's phonemic awareness that serves as an early indicator of how well and how easily he or she will learn to read, not phonics. "Since this is such a reliable indicator, and since rhymes are so naturally appealing to children this age, kindergarten classrooms should be filled with rhymes" (Cunningham 39). And although developmentally, rhyme and word patterns are especially critical for the primary classrooms, rhyme and rhythm should be a part of all instruction at all levels; they are basic to our language. For many reasons music and rhymes are natural resources for wordplay. They develop awareness of phoneme patterns and language possibilities within children's brains, serving as a metaphorical rubber chew toy for teething puppies. They sling it around, chew it up, and sharpen their bite. Without it, things tend to get messed up and usually only the puppy is punished.

Bringing music into the classroom is a powerful way to make learning meaningful and lasting. "The arts as ways of knowing are as potentially powerful as any other form of human discourse, and they are just as capable of contributing to the developing mind on a conceptual level" (Swanwick 48). Music provides students with a way to receive information that makes lasting connections. An old Chinese proverb explains, "Tell me, I'll forget. Show me, I may remember. Involve me, I'll understand."

Music involves students in making associations between the English language we wish them to learn more about and the language of music they already know and pay so much attention to daily. And as Peter Russell notes in *The Brain Book*, "The more associations we make when learning material, the easier it is to remember that material. Indeed, so powerful is the role of association that almost nothing will destroy it" (100).

Tone for Two

Rationale:

Music and different musical genres elicit a wide range of emotions. Words are a wonderful way to express the feelings evoked by various kinds of music. Through this activity, students explore the abstract concept of tone and/or mood through the connections found between music and written language. In this way, students gain a deeper understanding of adjectives and other parts of speech through meaningful context rather than as abstract concepts learned in isolation.

Objective:

Students will explore the abstract concept of tone and mood in both music and writing through the use of adjectives.

Materials:

Cash register tape (each student will need a strip approximately 15" long)
Colored markers
A variety of musical selections taped onto an audiotape or CD. Any songs that express a variety of tones will work. Suggested genres may include: jazz, rock, classical, new age, hip-hop, etc. Six selections on the tape or CD work nicely and allow flexibility with varying time schedules and lesson needs.
A tape player or CD player

Presentation Guidelines:

- Once students have their register tape and markers, explain that you are going to play some music selections. Explain that you do not want them to make any comments out loud or any judgments about the type of music. You only want them to write words and figurative phrases (for older students) that reflect the variety of feelings that each music clip evokes.

- Pausing briefly between each clip, play all samples. After the first clip and in the pauses between the others, ask a couple of students to share. This will assist students who may not be clear on the directions or what possible words they can use.

- After the listening portion of the lesson, students should share their strips of feelings with a peer.

- Students should then share the words and phrases they generated as a whole class. As they are shared, the words should be written on the board, a transparency, or on butcher paper.

- The responses are written in one of two columns drawn on the board (T-Chart). Any word that is an adjective should be written in the column on the left; all other words will be written in the column on the right. Unless the students mention it, do not tell them how the words are being divided.

- Once many (or all) examples have been placed on the board, ask students if they notice a pattern with the words in the left-hand column.

- Guide the discussion. More than likely, depending on their level and age, students will first say that the words on the left side describe "feelings." From there, guide them to remember that words that describe are *adjectives*. Adjectives are words that help explain the music's mood or tone. Some songs make you feel sad, for example, while others make you feel happy or exhilarated. There are certain musical patterns that composers can change to alter our feelings.

- Create another T-Chart. On the left side of the chart write "Musicians." As a class, brainstorm what musicians/composers alter in music that changes the audience's feelings. What was the difference in each of the selections that changed the listener's feelings? Write the responses on the left side of the chart in list format. Depending on the age, level, and musical background of the students, you may have to provide some of the terms (another great opportunity to introduce new vocabulary).

  A few possibilities:
  Minor keys for darker tones
  Major keys for lighter tones
  Density of instruments used
  Tempo/speed
  Types of instruments used
  Volume

- Then move to the other side of the chart and write "Writers" at the top of the column. Using the ideas generated about music, discuss what writers do to change feelings. How do writers change the tempo? How do writers change the volume? What do writers change that is like musicians changing between minor and major keys? (word choice, style of the writer, voice, format, vocabulary)

- The discussion may be high level, but students should be able to see the connections between music and writing and understand both tone and adjectives.

- To guide students toward application, ask them to locate a passage from a novel they are reading or from another piece of writing and discuss what tone is evident or what mood the reader experiences. It is important that students provide the evidence for their ideas. The discussion and evidence should be written in a paragraph format.

Evaluation/Variations:

- A grade can be given for the application paragraph and for the initial cash register feeling strip.

Moody Words

Rationale:

Pronouncing new words accurately is as important as knowing what the words mean. This activity is designed to enhance reading fluency and the use of the words in speech. This strategy focuses on pronunciation and should be combined with a strategy that focuses on definition. By repeating the words in a light, playful manner, students strengthen their episodic memory and can better remember the words and their pronunciation.

Objective:

Students will repeat a list of words using a variety of emotional tones and/or volumes to increase fluency and word recognition.

Materials:

List of words that will be learned through any vocabulary strategy

Presentation Guidelines:

- For the sake of explanation, assume the students are going to learn and study the following words. These words will create pronunciation problems for many students even if they successfully learn the definitions.

  chagrin   turgid   intrepid   tortuous   solace

- The Moody Words process will assist students with clear, accurate pronunciation. Say the first word clearly. Ask the students to repeat the word after you. Make sure the students can see the words as they are going through the process.

- Then ask the students to say the word as if they are sad. The emotion you choose to use does not matter. You will say the word with the tone of the chosen emotion first, and then the students will repeat after you.

- Continue in the same manner with each word on the list, using a different emotion, dialect, or volume for each. Say each word with three variations and then end by saying the words with normal speech. See list of moody possibilities below.

Evaluation/Variation:

- The evaluation, in this case, involves monitoring for proper pronunciation. If students are pronouncing the word incorrectly, model the accurate pronunciation again and ask them to repeat. The various tones provide motivation and energy.

30 Moody Possibilities

Ask students to say the word as if they are:

Sad
Happy
Bored
Tired
Out of breath
From England (or with any other accent)
Angry
In love
Hoarse
A baby
Telling a secret
Riding in a bumpy car
Scared
Singing
Melting
Surprised
A game announcer/sports broadcaster
Shy
A cheerleader
Sleepy
Lazy
A linebacker
Disappointed

Volumes/Tones/Tempos:
whisper
loudly
slow motion
quickly
high pitch
low pitch

**** *Note: Many of the Moody Possibilities words themselves create moments for advancing vocabulary.*

Radio Ga Ga

Rationale:

Ideally, students would use all newly acquired words immediately within a completely authentic writing or other context. However, the reality is that most students continue to use the words they are most comfortable with in their writing. As with all learning, moving new vocabulary words into writing requires scaffolding of the process and guided opportunities for application. Radio Ga Ga gives students a comfortable, creative setting in which to practice newly learned words. The novelty and energy of the activity serve to motivate students and increase their episodic memory.

Objective:

Students will write short text responses, using music as a stimulus. Students will be challenged to include words learned during a previous lesson or from a particular content area. The words selected should not be completely new

Materials:

A radio or CD player
A preselected list of words (or a list generated, through brainstorming, with the students)

Presentation Guidelines:

- The name of this activity alone is enough to pique students' interest. I have never worked with a group of students who were not intrigued when they walked into the room to see Radio Ga Ga written on the board.
- Explain that Radio Ga Ga will be used as a way to practice using less familiar words in our writing.
- On the board or overhead, list the words that will be included in the writing (between five and ten recently learned words).
- Use the Moody Word strategy from the previous Plug-in to make sure students know how to pronounce each word.
- Make sure the radio is set to an appropriate station. Some stations have commentators or music that may not be appropriate for the classroom setting. I like to use stations that the kids listen to.
- I prefer using the radio rather than a CD, however, because of the variety and unpredictability of phrases that will emerge.
- Turn the volume all the way down.

- Explain to students that you are going to turn the volume up and that they should write down whatever phrase or sentence (snippet) they hear.
- This will then serve as the starting point for everyone's writing, which will then incorporate the vocabulary word(s). Every once in a while, the phrase or sentence will not be useable; it is fine to turn the volume down and try again. If at all possible, use the snippet or a portion of the snippet that is heard.
- The fun aspect is that the phrase or sentence may be part of a song, news coverage, an advertisement, or a conversation.
- I was working on this activity with a sixth-grade class. The first snippet that was heard was "*Do you think you're better off alone?*" Initially we did not incorporate the vocabulary words. I wanted them to understand how Radio Ga Ga worked before they tried weaving in the words.
- Students wrote for only two to three minutes from that snippet. The challenge, for the next round, was to use one or more of the vocabulary words within their Radio Ga Ga.

Christine Schweter, a sixth-grade student, wrote:

- Depending on the snippet, the tone of the writing may end up serious, silly, humorous, philosophical, sad, etc. This is a wonderful opportunity to introduce or readdress the concept of tone. It is wonderful to observe the different responses students have to the same snippet. Even very young writers do a wonderful job with this activity.
- Allow a couple of students to share their responses. Before each student begins reading, have him or her disclose which vocabulary word(s) was used so that students can listen for it.
- Repeat the process at least one more time. Ask students to use different vocabulary words for each snippet.

Evaluation/Variations:

- The grading is simple for the vocabulary component. If the student used the word(s) accurately within the response, then credit is given. Other criteria may be required, depending on what you have taught.

- I use the Radio Ga Ga responses throughout the year for more than just vocabulary application. I use students' responses also for spelling, grammar, punctuation, and sentence structure mini-lessons.

- I have also, with success, changed Radio Ga Ga to Story Ga Ga. The process is the same except the snippets come from books on tape. (Public libraries and education service centers have many wonderful children's books and young adult books on tape.)

Chapter 7

Plugging In Poetry

*"A poet is only as sharp as his tools, and a wordsmith with a
limited vocabulary is bound to be dull."*

–Nikki Grimes

In my eyes, my grandmother was famous. I loved lying on the floor of her living room with her scrapbook open before me, its ancient cellophane tape cracking and peeling away from the newspaper clippings, which were yellowed with the breath of time. The clippings came from the *Austin American Statesman*, where my grandmother's poems had frequently been published. I had read them so many times that I could lie in bed at night and recite them by heart. Some were serious, some religious or philosophical, but it was the light-hearted, humorous poems that I loved best.

More than reading the poems, however, I loved sitting with her in her front yard in metal rocking lawn chairs, creating our own poems. The afternoons slipped away as my grandmother and I played with words. Little did she or I know, at the time, the benefits this play would have on my language development. She could not have known the patterns for words she wove into my brain or the love of language imbedded into my heart.

Well-written poetry is concise, precise, and contains important language elements that, like music, create a kind of pleasing harmony when read out loud. Bob Holman, coeditor of *Aloud: Voices from the Nuyorican Poets Café* explains, "Poetry is a contact sport." The contacts it makes are numerous. Both reading and writing poetry enhance the study of words. "Good poetry requires precision; if you do not attempt to say accurately, truthfully, what you feel or need, then how will you achieve precision? What criterion will guide you to the next absolutely 'right' word?" (Muller 3).

Poetry demands accuracy of language, which gives birth to clarity of thought. This is a genre that rarely receives enough serious attention in many classrooms. It is seen as "extra," something to squeeze in if time permits after all of the standardized tests have been completed. But poetry helps develop students' ear for language. My mantra to the teachers and students I work with is that poetry is not a unit; it is the heartbeat of language and literacy.

Perhaps we need to make sure that no genre is left behind. Poetic elements can be found in almost every writing genre, and other genres and critical conventions of writing are intricately woven within the lines of poetry. Teachers must read poetry themselves to be able to choose poets and selections that enhance word study. The objectives to be taught drive the selection process. The poem must add depth to the concepts, skills, or patterns being explored.

When we look at a well-constructed poem, the precision of the words used enhances the discussion of word choice and the writer's voice. As Laurence Perrine explains in *Sound and Sense*, "A frequent misconception of poetic language is that poets seek always the most beautiful or noble sounding words. What they really seek are the most meaningful words, and these vary from one context to another" (40). When writing poems, students are exploring language at the connotative, denotative, and sound pattern levels. The word meanings are not simply black and white. The kaleidoscope of possibilities allows students to knead the meaning into the ideal shape and form. "In fact, the many varieties of language open to poets provide their richest resource; creating poems requires constant exploration and discovery. They search always for the secret affinities of words that allows them to be brought together with soft explosions of meaning" (Perrine 40).

Words can have many layers of meaning, and poetry allows the writer and the reader to peel away layer after layer of possible meanings. These multiple possibilities force students to examine the layers and, depending on the context, make a decision on the meaning being used by the author of a text or the meaning needing to be used when composing a piece. These examinations of meaning occur both consciously and subconsciously.

The more word and text experience students have, the more easily and quickly they can make decisions—which leads to increasing fluency and comprehension. "There is no poem that can live, come alive, without a reader. The reader, the listener, breathes into each work of art his own experience, his own sensitivity, and re-creates it in meaningful terms" (Livingston 207). In that recreation comes true learning and deep retention of words.

Word Slam

Rationale:

Poetry slams have been gaining in popularity for many years. From the open-mike slams at the Nuyorican Poets Café in New York to similar events held at small cafés, coffee shops, and bookstores across the country, the sound of words is luring audiences of all ages to stop and listen. "How do writers learn the weight of words? From childhood, they read and are read to; they read more and listen; they listen to the language the way artists look at paintings" (MacNeil 225). Word Slams provide a gallery of sound—ear training, if you will—for students so they can learn to listen and weigh words, giving them hope of being able to pause, reflect, and appreciate that an author used *sauntered* as opposed to *walked*, or used *walked* because it was, in fact, the perfect word.

Objective:

Students will learn the elements of the spoken word genre and create poems to read out loud. Though topics for poems written for poetry slams vary, as with any other genre, students will, for the Word Slam, write poems about specific words.

Materials:

Selected resources to model spoken word genre (see 100 Plus Poetry Picks at the end of this chapter)

Many CDs are available for spoken word and numerous websites now focus on poetry slams and open-mike readings (you must review these materials and sites carefully for appropriate content)

Props and materials needed to host your class's own Word Slam

Michaela Gilbert, 6th Grader, Drew Academy;
Houston, Texas

Presentation Guidelines:

- Discuss with students the fact that poetry began as an oral tradition. Our earliest poems, such as *Beowulf* and the *Odyssey*, were read out loud to entertain as audiences listened.

- Provide a printed copy of a spoken word poem that you have available on tape or CD. Ask students to silently read the poem. For the purpose of contrast, it is important that students first read the poem silently.

- Then play the recorded version of the selection out loud.

- As a class, brainstorm and discuss the differences between the two readings. This discussion is crucial to help students understand and appreciate the importance of exploring words and language patterns through the sense of hearing rather than simply through sight. Frank Smith, in *Reading Without Nonsense*, explains the neurological reality that the eyes merely look; it is the brain that perceives and sees. The ears enhance the brain's ability to perceive many more layers of possible meanings.

- Play a few more examples of spoken word poems, pointing out techniques the writers used to provide a sense of rhythm.

- Provide a list of difficult words (and/or content-based words) for students to select from.

- Each student will choose a different word. I have allowed students to work in pairs; this decision is, of course, at the discretion of the teacher.

- Students should then be given time to explore the word. (See Sound Board on page 110) To effectively write a poem focusing on one word requires detailed information about the selected word.

- Incorporating the entire writing process, including revision and editing, scaffold students through the writing of a spoken word poem. Peer feedback is a crucial aspect of this process.

- Once the poems have been written, conduct an open-mike Word Slam reading. My sixth-grade class invited teachers and other faculty members to observe and participate. We created the atmosphere of a coffeehouse: students brought favorite coffee mugs and we served hot chocolate and cookies.

- The learning that occurred throughout the process was amazing. However, on the day of the actual Word Slam, the exposure to and sampling of words was prodigious. The teacher's involvement in modeling the process is one of the most critical instructional elements when exploring and listening to words.

Alana Morris shares an open mike poem with her sixth grade students at Drew Academy.

Evaluation/Variations:

- Feedback and evaluation occur throughout the Word Slam experience. However, for the final Word Slam performance, a rubric should be created, focusing on all of the elements taught through the writing process.

- Vocabulary words provide only one way to use the Word Slam. Poetry slams are great venues for writing and presenting content-area poems, or just to allow students to explore language through this popular genre.

Sound Board
Planning Page

Word:

Facts about your word: (part of speech, synonyms, antonyms, homonyms, origins, etc.)

Uses for this word: (In what contexts might it be used and by whom?)

Figurative language: (How can the word be described figuratively?)

Words that sound great with your word: (Alliteration, repetition, rhyme, etc.)

Other brilliant ideas:

Title Quest

Rationale:

Inference is a reading skill that demands constant attention. In order to become aware of the inferences we make and to scaffold the invisible skill of inferencing, teachers must model and think aloud this complex process. Words create the ultimate inference experience. If required skills for reading were separated out into rides for a major theme park, inference would be the grandest, most thrilling roller coaster ever created. Whether we're inferring time, locations, character motive, cause and effect relationships, or numerous other possibilities, the secret sleeps behind the words.

When detectives examine the scene of a crime, even though many objects are at the scene, some items catch the attention of their well-trained senses, while others do not. The same is true for readers and text. Some words deserve reflection and weight; others simply serve as the mortar that holds the ideas in place as the text moves along. Title Quest helps the reader gain understanding of how one word or phrase merits greater weight than another. Furthermore, the process not only marks time within the text, giving pause to certain words over those that are less important, but also requires high-level synthesis and the expression of ideas through writing with textual evidence.

Objectives:

Students will use inferencing and generalizing skills to determine what they think the title of a text is, based on words (evidence) from within the text. Likewise, students will discover that some words carry more weight than others within a text.

Materials:

Poems, articles, textbook chapters, or other reading materials. Due to the precision and concise nature of words used, I prefer to use poems initially in this activity.

Presentation Guidelines:

- Pre-select a poem that contains key words that would give students clues necessary to determine the title. The thinking process for this activity is more important than accurately coming up with the title.
- Share the following guidelines with the students:

  1. The selection (if orally shared) will be read two times.
  2. The first time the poem is read, students should listen carefully for the general idea of the text and should begin to infer/predict what the author chose as a title for the selection.
  3. During the second reading, students should look for textual clues (words) to serve as supporting evidence for their idea(s).

- On a sheet of notebook paper, students will write down what they believe is the title of the poem. You may give a hint by telling them how many words are in the title. If they ask, I often share whether or not the title appears in the actual text.
- Once students have written down their inferred title, they should provide evidence from the text to support their answer.
- Allow a few students to share their responses and evidence prior to taking up their answers and/or sharing the actual title.
- Share with the students the actual title of the poem.
- If time permits, it is beneficial to reread the text and have a student write key words and phrases on the board as they come up within the reading. This will reemphasize and model the process for students.
- Again, many students will give excellent title suggestions and excellent evidence from the text, even though they do not come up with the exact title the author used. Validate these responses as good answers supported by good thinking. Often some student titles are more logical than the published title. Another side benefit of this strategy is that it helps students explore what makes a good title, and to avoid flat ones like *My View on World Peace*.

Evaluation/Variation(s):

- I actually give students bonus points if they get the exact title the author wrote, but I want to emphasize that the objective is not necessarily to get the exact "right" answer. The goal is for the students to do the thinking and to gather the text evidence provided to support that thinking.
- I decide how many bonus points to award (up to five) based on how many students get the title right. The more students who get it right, the fewer points it is worth. This is a fun challenge for the students and motivates them not to share their answers with their peers. If they were to share, they would get fewer points.

Snip-It Word Poems

Adapted from my colleague Steve Anderson, who sadly enough has left the teaching profession.

Rationale:

Often vocabulary study is seen as merely looking up previously unknown, complex words to acquire definitions. But vocabulary growth requires a far deeper lexical experience. Students who score well on standardized tests in the vocabulary area are students who typically score well across the board in language, and these students *own* the words they use, they understand relationships between words, and their in-depth understanding of language allows them to analyze the word parts and to discard the distracters they are given as answer choices on assessments. Exposure to words can come in many forms. Snip-It Word Poems give students an opportunity to find interesting words, analyze those words, and then synthesize selected words into a meaningful format.

Students must have a good understanding of the selected words to create the poem. Another benefit is the review of parts of speech in a meaningful way. All students at all levels can have success with this activity. The complexity of the poem will vary, depending on the words students select, but the benefit remains the same. A second grader's poem may be extremely concrete, while an older student's poem may be philosophical and abstract. The learning is in the process.

Objective:

Students will select 30 words from magazines (the number of words can be altered if needed). The words will consist of nouns, verbs, articles, interjections, adjectives, adverbs, and prepositions. Words will range from one to four syllables. The chosen words will be arranged into a poem and glued onto construction paper. Students should be able to provide definitions for all words selected.

Materials:

Scissors
Glue
Magazines
Construction paper
Markers

Presentation Guidelines:

- Share with students that poems come in many formats, but one characteristic that all poems have in common is carefully selected words. One subgenre of poetry is the found poem. There are many forms of found poems. Annie Dillard has even used class notes to create found poetry (see her book *Mornings Like This*).

- Using an overhead of the Snip-It Collection Guide (see page 115), model how the students will search through magazines to find the required words. Model how the best words to select are words that will sound good together. Students' poems will not come out as well if they haphazardly select words or just select the first words they come across. Often students like to locate words that follow a particular theme.

- Once students understand the process, let them begin searching through the magazines with their own Snip-It Collection Guide.

- By the end of the day, I have finished my own poem to publish along with those of my class. It is important to experience the process yourself in order to effectively model and scaffold the process with students.

- Once the words have been collected, it is important to then model the process of arranging the collected words into a poem. Encourage students to focus on patterns and rhythms rather than rhyme. They should read the possibilities out loud before reaching for the glue. The ear must give full approval before students think about gluing the words down on paper. Once the ears are impressed, then the eyes get to make sure the arrangement is acceptable. There are many possibilities for how the words are placed on the page (four lines, eight lines, stanzas, etc.). Tell students that even the way the words are arranged on the page provides meaning for the poem. Poets carefully choose where they break a line of poetry. **Ten handwritten (filler) words can be used, if needed, to join the magazine words together.**

- Publish the students' Snip-it Word Poems after they have shared them out loud.

Evaluation/Variations:

- I typically give two grades for the Snip-It Word Poem. One grade is given for the collection guide and one for the final poem.

- Rather than cutting words out of magazines, students can select words and/or phrases from other sources, such as the novels they are reading, their textbooks, their own compositions, or printed texts from elsewhere around the school (signs, posters, trophy cases, etc.).

Snip-It Collection Guide

Using the magazines from the room, locate the following 30 words for your poem:

NOUNS: (11)	3 one syllable	3 two syllable	1 three syllable	1 four syllable	3 pronouns
	1.	1.			1.
	2.	2.			2.
	3.	3.			3.

Verbs: (5)	2 of any type of verb	3 multi-syllable verbs
	1.	1.
	2.	2.
		3.

Adjectives: (5)	2 one syllable	1 two syllable	1 three syllable	1 four syllable
	1.			
	2.			

Adverbs:	Prepositions	Articles	1 Interjection
1.	1.	1.	
2.	2.	2.	
	3.	3.	

100 Plus Poetry Picks for all Ages

> *** Denotes that mature language or content appears in some poems in the collection and reader/teacher discretion is advised. These resources should not be left out in the classroom.
>
> ♫ Denotes Spoken Word Poetry Resource
>
> 📖 Denotes a Young Adult Novel that focuses on Spoken Word Poetry
>
> ✋ Denotes a Poetry Book especially appropriate for, but not limited to, Young Readers

Alarcon, Francisco X. 1997. *Laughing Tomatoes and Other Spring Poems*. San Francisco, California: Children's Book Press. ✋

Anglesey, Zoe (edited). 1999. *Listen Up: Spoken Word Poetry*. New York, New York: Ballantine Publishing Group. ♫ ***

Appelt, Kathi. 1996. *Just People and other Poems for Young Readers*. Spring, Texas: Absey & Co.

Applet, Kathi. 2002. *Poems from Homeroom: A Writer's Place to Start*. New York, New York: Henry Holt and Company.

Baca, Jimmy Santiago. 1989. *Black Mesa Poems*. New York, New York: New Directions Publisher.

Bagert, Brod. 2002. *Giant Children*. New York, New York: Dial Books for Young Readers. ✋

Bagert, Brod. 1999. *Rainbows, Head Lice, and Pea-Green Tile: Poems in the Voice of the Classroom Teacher*. Gainesville, Florida: Maupin House Publishing.

Bearden, Romare and Langston Hughes. 1995. *The Block*. New York, New York: Viking Books.

Blum, Joshua, et. al. 1996. *The United States of Poetry*. New York, New York: Harry N. Abrams, Inc., Publishers. *** ♫

Bowman, Catherine. 2003. *Word of Mouth: Poems Featured on NPR's All Things Considered*. New York, New York: Vintage Books.

Carlson, Lori M. (editor). 1994. *Cool Salsa: Bilingual Poems on Growing up Latino in the United States*. New York, New York: Fawcett Juniper.

Carroll, Joyce Armstrong and Eddie Wilson (compiled). 1997. *Poetry After Lunch: Poems to Read Aloud*. Spring, Texas: Absey & Co.

Collins, Billy (selected). 2003. *Poetry 180: A Turning Back to Poetry*. New York: Random House.

Collins, Billy. 2001. *Sailing Alone Around the Room*. New York, New York: Random House.

Dakos, Kalli. 1993. *Don't Read This Book Whatever You Do: More Poems About School*. New York: Four Winds Press. ♥

Dakos, Kalli. 1990. *If You're Not Here, Please Raise Your Hand: Poems About School*. New York, New York: Four Winds Press. ♥

Dakos, Kalli. 2003. *Put Your Eyes Up Here and other School Poems*. New York, New York: Simon and Schuster Books for Young Readers. ♥

Daniels, Jim (edited). 1995. *Letters to America: Contemporary American Poetry on Race*. Detroit, Michigan: Wayne State University Press.

Dillard, Annie. 1995. *Mornings Like This: Found Poems*. New York, New York: Harper Perennial.

Dunning, Stephen, et. al. (compiled). 1995. *Reflections on a Gift of Watermelon Pickle...and other Modern Verse*. Glenview, Illinois: Scott Foresman.

Eleveld, Mark. 2003. *The Spoken Word Revolution (Slam, Hip Hop & the Poetry of a New Generation) and [CD]*. Naperville, Illinois: Sourcebooks, Inc. *** ♫

Esbensen, Barbara Juster. 1995. *Dance With Me*. New York, New York: Harper Collins Publishers. ♥

Esbensen, Barbara Juster. 1986. *Words with Wrinkled Knees*. Honesdale, Pennsylvania: Boyds Mill Press. ♥

Fleischman, Paul. 2000. *Big Talk: Poems for Four Voices*. Cambridge, Massachusetts: Candlewick Press. ♥

Fleischman, Paul. 1988. *Joyful Noise: Poems for Two Voices*. New York, New York: Harper Trophy. ♥

Florian, Douglas. 1998. *Insectlopedia*. San Diego, California: Harcourt Brace and Company. ♥

Gendler, Ruth. 1988. *The Book of Qualities*. New York, New York: Harper Perennial.

George, Kristine O'Connell. 2002. *Swimming Upstream: Middle School Poems*. New York: Clarion Books.

Giovanni, Nikki. 1978. *Cotton Candy on a Rainy Day*. New York: Quill Books.

Graves, Donald. 1996. *Baseball, Snakes, and Summer Squash: Poems About Growing Up*. Honesdale, Pennsylvania: Boyds Mills Press. ♥

Greenberg, Jan. 2001. *Heart to Heart: New Poems Inspired by Twentieth-Century American Art*. New York, New York: Harry N. Abrams, Inc.

Grimes, Nikki. 1998. *A Dime a Dozen*. New York: Dial Books.

Grimes, Nikki. 2002. *Bronx Masquerade*. New York: Dial Books. 📖 ♫

Grimes, Nikki. 1999. *My Man Blue*. New York, New York: Dial Books.

High, Linda Oatman. 2004. *Sister Slam and the Poetic Motormouth Road Trip*. New York, New York: Bloomsbury USA Children's Books. ♫ 📖

Hindley, Judy. 1998. *A Song of Colors*. Cambridge, Massachusetts: Candlewick Press. ♥

Hopkins, Lee Bennett (selected). 1993. *Extra Innings: Baseball Poems*. San Diego, California: Harcourt Brace Jovanovich, Publishers.

Hopkins, Lee Bennett (selected). 1990. *Good Books, Good Times!* New York, New York: HarperCollins Publishers. ♥

Hopkins, Lee Bennett (selected). 1997. *Marvelous Math: A Book of Poems*. New York, New York: Simon and Schuster Books for Young Readers. ♥

Hopkins, Lee Bennett (selected). 2000. *My America: A Poetry Atlas of the United States*. New York, New York: Simon and Schuster Books for Young Readers.

Hopkins, Lee Bennett (selected). 1997. *Song and Dance*. New York, New York: Simon and Schuster Books for Young Readers. ♥

Hopkins, Lee Bennett (selected). 2004. *Wonderful Words: Poems about Reading, Writing, Speaking, and Listening*. New York, New York: Simon and Schuster Books for Young Readers.

Igus, Toyomi. 1998. *I See the Rhythm*. San Francisco, California: Children's Book Press.

Intrator, Sam M. and Megan Scribner (editors). 2003. *Teaching With Fire: Poetry that Sustain the Courage to Teach*. San Francisco, California: Jossey-Bass.

Janeczko, Paul (selected). *A Poke in the I: A Collection of Concrete Poems*. Cambridge, Massachusetts: Candlewick Press.

Janeczko, Paul (selected). 2001. *Dirty Laundry Pile: Poems in Different Voices*. New York: Harper Collins Publishers. ♥

Janeczko, Paul (selected). 1993. *Looking for Your Name: A Collection of Contemporary Poems*.

Janeczko, Paul (compiled). 1994. *Poetry from A to Z: A Guide for Young Writers*. New York: Bradbury Press.

Janeczko, Paul (selected). 1983. *Poetspeak*. New York, New York: Collier Books.

Janeczko, Paul (compiled). 2002. *Seeing the Blue Between: Advice and Inspiration for Young Poets*. Cambridge, Massachusetts: Candlewick Press.

Janeczko, Paul (selected). 2000. *Stone Bench in an Empty Park*. New York, New York: Orchard Books.

Janeczko, Paul (selected). 1984. *Strings: A Gathering of Family Poems*. New York: Bradbury Press.

Janeczko, Paul (selected). 1990. *The Place My Words are Looking For*. New York: Macmillan Books for Young Readers.

Janeczko, Paul (selected). 1995. *Wherever Home Begins: 100 Contemporary Poems*. New York, New York: Orchard Books.

Koch, Kenneth and Kate Farrell. 1981. *Sleeping on the Wing: An Anthology of Modern Poetry with Essays on Reading and Writing*. New York: Vintage Books.

Little, Jean. 1986. *Hey World, Here I am!* New York: Trumpet Club. ♥

Livingston, Myra Cohn (selected). 1997. *I am Writing a Poem About...: A Game About Poetry*. New York, New York: Margaret K. McElderry Books.

Lyon, George Ella. 1999. *Where I'm From*. Spring, Texas: Absey & Co.

Medearis, Angela Shelf. 1995. *Skin Deep and Other Teenage Reflections*. New York, New York: Macmillan Books for Young Readers.

Medina, Jane. 1999. *My Name is Jorge on Both Sides of the River*. Honesdale, Pennsylvania: Boyds Mills Press, Inc. ♥

Mora, Pat. 1986. *Borders*. Houston, Texas. Arte Publico Press.

Mora, Pat. 1996. *Confetti: Poems for Children*. New York, New York: Lee & Low Books. ♥

Mora, Pat. 2000. *My Own True Name: New and Selected Poems for Young Adults*. Houston, Texas: Pinata Books.

Morrison, Lillian (compiled). 1995. *Slam Dunk: Basketball Poems*. New York: Hyperion Books for Children.

Nelson, Marilyn. 2001. *Carver: A Life in Poems*. New York: Scholastic, Inc.

Neruda, Pablo. 1994. *Ode to Common Things*. Boston: Little Brown and Company.

Neruda, Pablo. 1974. *The Book of Questions*. Port Townsend, Washington: Copper Canyon Press.

Nicholls, Judith (compiled). 2000. *Someone I Like: Poems About People*. New York: Bare Foot Books. ♥

Nordine, Ken. 2000. *Colors*. San Diego, California: Harcourt Brace Jovanovich. ♫

Nordine, Ken. 2000. *Colors* [CD]. #954. San Francisco, California: Asphodel Records. ♫

Numeroff, Laura. 1999. *Sometimes I Wonder if Poodles Like Noodles*. New York, New York: Simon and Schuster Books for Young Readers.

Nye, Naomi Shihab. 2000. *Come With Me: Poems for a Journey*. New York, New York: Greenwillow Books.

Nye, Naomi Shihab. 1998. *Fuel: Poems by Naomi Shihab Nye*. New York, New York: Boa Editions, Ltd.

Nye, Naomi Shihab and Paul B. Janeczko. 1996. *I Feel a Little Jumpy Around You: A Book of Her Poems & His Poems Collected in Pairs*. New York, New York: Simon and Schuster Books for Young Readers.

Nye, Naomi Shihab. 2004. *Is This Forever or What?: Poems & Paintings from Texas*. New York, New York: Greenwillow Books.

Nye, Naomi Shihab. 1994. *Red Suitcase*. Brockport, New York: BOA Editions, Ltd.

Nye, Naomi Shihab (selected). 2000. *Salting the Ocean: 100 Poems by Young Poets*. New York, New York: Greenwillow Books.

Nye, Naomi Shihab (selected). 1998. *The Space Between Our Footsteps: Poems and Paintings form the Middle East*. New York, New York: Simon and Schuster Books for Young Readers.

Nye, Naomi Shihab (selected). 1992. *This Same Sky: A Collection of Poems from Around the World*. New York: Four Winds Press.

Nye, Naomi Shihab. 1995. *Words Under the Words*. Portland, Oregon: The Eighth Mountain Press.

O'Neill, Mary. 1961. *Hailstones and Halibut Bones: Adventures in Color*. New York: Doubleday. ♥

Paschen, Elise and Rebekah Presson Mosby (editors). 2001. *Poetry Speaks: Hear Great Poets Read Their Work from Tennyson to Plath*. Naperville, Illinois: Sourcebooks, Inc. ♫

Robb, Laura (selected). 1997. *Music and Drum: Voices of War and Peace, Hope and Dreams*. New York, New York: Philomel Books.

Rochelle, Belinda (selected). 2001. *Words With Wings: A Treasury of African American Poetry and Art.* New York: Harper Collins Publishers.

Rodriguz, Luis J. 1998. *Trochemoche.* Connecticut: Curbstone Press. ***

Rylant, Cynthia. 1984. *Waiting to Waltz: A Childhood.* New York, New York: Macmillan Books for Young Readers.

Schertle, Alice. 1996. *Keepers.* New York, New York: Lothrop, Lee & Shepard Books. ✋

Shange, Ntozake. 1994. *I Live in Music.* New York, New York: Welcome Enterprises, Inc.

Simmons, Danny and M. Raven Rowe (edited). *Russell Simmon's Def Poetry Jam on Broadway...and More.* New York, New York: Atria Books. *** ♫

Singer, Marilyn. 1996. *All We Needed to Say: Poems about School from Tanya and Sophie.* New York, New York: Atheneum Books for Young Readers.

Smith, Charles R. Jr. 1999. *Rimshots: Basketball Pix, Rolls, and Rhythms.* New York, New York: Dutton Children's Books.

Soto, Gary. 1995. *Canto Familiar.* San Diego, California: Harcourt Brace and Company.

Soto, Gary. 2002. *Fearless Fernie: Hanging out with Fernie and Me.* New York: G.P. Putnam's Sons.

Soto, Gary. 1992. *Neighborhood Odes.* New York, New York: Scholastic, Inc.

Soto, Gary. 1990. *Who Will Know Us?* San Francisco, California: Chronicle Books.

Steptoe, Javaka. 1997. *In Daddy's Arms I am Tall: African Americans Celebrating Fathers.* New York, New York: Lee & Low Books, Inc.

Stevenson, James. 1995. *Sweet Corn.* New York, New York: Greenwillow Books. ✿

Swados, Elizabeth. 2002. *Hey You! C'Mere: A Poetry Slam.* New York, New York: Scholastic, Inc.

The United States of Poetry Soundtrack [CD]. (1996). 532139. New York, New York: Polygram Records. *** ♫

Von Ziegesar, Cecily. 2000. *Slam.* New York, New York: Alloy Books.

Whipple, Laura. 2002. *If the Shoe Fits: Voices from Cinderella.* New York, New York: Margaret K. Mclderry Books.

Wong, Janet. 2003. *Knock on Wood: Poems About Superstitions.* New York, New York: Margaret K. McElderry Books.

Chapter 8
Plugging In Context

"Theories that suggest that we learn best when we break a task down into discrete parts do not really make possible the sort of learning that is accomplished through mindful awareness of distinctions."

—Ellen Langer

Much research in the area of language study has been devoted to the acquisition and use of new vocabulary words. The studies are varied and complex, but generally they support multiple instructional methods and recommend a multidimensional, balanced approach to word study, including formal instruction in morphological knowledge, learning individual word meanings via definitions, providing the new word in context, and deriving word meanings from context.

The research in the area of cognition and language indicates that the human brain is naturally wired to acquire new words; the perplexing question remains, however, as to why such great individual differences in students' word knowledge persist even after formal vocabulary instruction and environmental exposure to new words.

As discussed in Chapter Two: Plugging in Memory, many answers lie within our complex human memory systems. Alan Baddeley, an expert in this field, explains, "Close links have been established between children's phonological memory abilities and both their native language vocabulary knowledge and their second language learning… In particular, the ease of learning new words seems to be limited by the adequacy of an individual's phonological memory system" (Gathercole and Baddeley 67).

Without going too deeply into the vast amount of research in this area, we can say definitely that a critical component for creating strong memory traces and moving new words to long-term memory is context. One of the most significant ways of deriving context for new words is, of course, through reading. Studies conducted by researchers such as Stanovich and Cunningham (1991) show that individual differences in children's vocabulary knowledge are predictable on the basis of how familiar the students are with book titles. Numerous studies support the idea that reading increases word knowledge and enhances other areas of language application such as grammar, sentence structures, and spelling.

Contextualization is important for any type of learning and is a major aspect of constructivist models of learning in particular. Unfortunately, word study, from phonics to traditional vocabulary study, has often been far removed from meaningful contexts. But it has been shown that our memories for information (such as new words) are strengthened when we are learning that information within a meaningful context. Likewise, using words, whether in spoken or written form, always requires a context. "People do not just blurt out isolated words but rather combine them into phrases and sentences, in which the meaning of the combination can be inferred from the meanings of the words and the way they are arranged" (Pinker 4).

Context provides students with opportunities to extract patterns. Patterns, as we have seen, are crucial for learning and help to move concepts to the application level. By providing rich, meaningful contexts, we will help students apply and retain the words they are attempting to learn, not just for a moment in standardized time, but to truly own the words for a lifetime.

Mental Mingling

Lesson adapted from Dr. Kelley Barger's lesson *The Dots Have It*

Rationale:

As important as context is for building strong memory traces, teaching students to use the context to shape their ideas of meaning is also important. Natural connoisseurs of language will automatically use context to bring meaning to unknown words. Struggling or less experienced language users will need more scaffolded guidance into the process of using context clues. This strategy, through interaction and movement, provides students with the opportunity and motivation to strengthen the skills required for sifting meaning from context.

Objective:

Students will explore the meaning of words through contexts in an interactive way.

Materials:

Post-it notes 3 x 5 size or larger for younger students
Index cards
Trade books, young adult novels, or other reading materials
Highlighting strips (Hotcover Book Covers cut into .5" x 1" strips work well. Store bought highlighting strips can be expensive)

Presentation Guidelines:

- Read a pre-selected portion of a young adult novel or trade book that has one or more challenging words in it. It is important to choose real text with a word that even you as the teacher may find challenging.

  Example: from *Harry Potter and the Sorcerer's Stone* by J. K. Rowling, chapter 16, paragraph 17

  "Harry was quite sure the unsettled feeling didn't have anything to do with work, though. He watched an owl flutter toward the school across the bright blue sky, a note clamped in its mouth. Hagrid was the only one who ever sent him letters. Hagrid would never *betray* Dumbledore. Hagrid would never tell anyone how to get past Fluffy…"

  I was careful to choose an example where context clues were clearly present.

- After sharing the selected word (betray), ask students how the reader might determine what the word means without stopping to look the word up in the dictionary. Several answers will be given. One or more students will offer the idea of context clues. Depending on the grade and/or level, you may have to lead students toward the idea of context clues.

- One instructional problem I have seen in many classrooms is the assumption that students understand the abstract terms-context and clues. Before proceeding with the lesson, discuss these terms to whatever degree is required for clear understanding.

- Model the process of placing the selected word, in this case *betray*, on the Post-it note. Only one single word should appear on the Post-it note. The students should make sure the word is spelled accurately and written neatly.

- Then, with the students' input, model and think aloud the process of deciding what the word means based on the context in which the word appeared. Model the process of writing the inferred meaning neatly on the index card.

- Give the class ten to fifteen minutes to read their novels/books. As they read, students should use highlighting strips (word darts) to mark words whose definitions are unfamiliar to them.

- At this time, students should not do anything with the Post-it notes or index cards. It is important that they continue to read for comprehension. Too many tasks that divide their attention will weaken or completely break down comprehension.

- Once the reading time has ended, ask students to select only one of their marked words for the activity (some students may have marked only one word, or in rare instances, may not have found a challenging word to mark). I request that any student who does not have a word marked find the most challenging word possible in the text he or she has read so far in the selected novel, trade book, or other reading materials.

- Students will now follow the same procedure you modeled earlier with the Post-it notes and the index cards.

- Once students have written the word on the Post-it note and their inferred definition on the index card, ask them to write their names on their index cards and then pass them in.

- Students should place the Post-it notes on their own backs.

- After the index cards have been mixed up, they will be redistributed, making sure students do not get their own card.

- The next portion of the lesson requires some preplanned management. I like to use the analogy of a nice dinner party or get-together. I ask students what "mingling" means. Rather than having multiple conversations as they mingle around the room, I suggest that our mingling for this activity will be "Mental Mingling." Students will not talk to one another as they mingle around the room trying to match the inferred definition from the card they receive to a Post-it note on one of their peers' backs.

- I play a classical music selection as they mingle-mentally, of course.

- Once students have found a match, they should take the Post-it note, stick it to the index card, and then have a seat. Allow time for most of the students to find a match for their index card.
- It is often the case that the words and definitions do not all accurately match. This is where the discussion and optimal instruction occur.
- Ask students to brainstorm possible reasons that all of the words and definitions do not match.
  –definition not accurate
  –someone took the wrong word for their definition
- As a class, make appropriate changes to correct any mismatches.

Evaluation/Variations:

- Grades can be given for the original context definition given on the index card and/or the matched card and Post-it note after the mingling. The learning from this activity is in the process. Monitoring and feedback should be offered throughout the learning episode.
- Mental Mingling can be used to review any previously learned vocabulary words.
- The Mental Mingling strategy can be used to practice math concepts as well. Place value review works exceptionally well.

On the Post-it note, students write a number that contains a decimal. You will pre-set the boundaries for the number (number of digits, etc.). Students underline one of the numbers.

On the index card, students will write out the value of the underlined number.

The Mental Mingling process remains the same. Students try to match up the underlined digit to the written value.

Eight one-hundredths	37.4<u>8</u>2

- The Mental Mingling strategy can also be used to review concepts for science, social studies, or any other content or co-curricular area.

Word Portfolios

Rationale:

Artists, models, graphic designers, writers, and many other professionals keep portfolios of their work in order to share with others the variety, diversity, and strength of what they've done. By keeping word portfolios, students are able to explore and study particular words in greater depth by discovering the variety, diversity, and strength of how words are applied in different contexts. Depth, once again, is the goal of this activity. Rather than simply learning the words and definitions, students are seeking out the context(s) in which the words are used. The learning from this activity is multilayered.

Objective:

Students will design and keep a word portfolio for a set time period. At the close of that time period, students will create a gallery displaying the samples that have been collected.

Materials:

Paper sacks (lunch bags work well)
Index cards
Velcro
Markers, colors, etc.
Poster board
Word Portfolio Guidelines for each student (Wording will need to be altered for younger students)
Resources for vocabulary words: www.freevocabulary.com, www.dictionary.com (word of the day), Kappan *Word Power* (see bibliography)

Presentation Guidelines:

- Have a brief discussion with students about portfolios. Brainstorm different professions that might keep portfolios (models, artists, photographers, writers, real estate agents, etc.).
- Ask students how, as words users, they might keep a word portfolio.
- Initially students will focus on one word only. Provide a list of high-level words. I like to use SAT words or other advanced lists. A great resource for such words is www.freevocabulary.com, but the source of the words does not matter. For younger students, emotion or character trait words are great to use.
- Let the students select the word for their portfolio since they will be spending quite a bit of time with this exploration.

- Explain that the word portfolio will be expanded, for the most part, outside of class time.
- Give the students a handout with all of the guidelines, expectations, and due dates. I have provided a sample that can be altered as needed. (See page 130).
- Making the portfolio is a great starting point for the exploration. The students will use the paper sacks to make their portfolios. Sigrid Yates, now an administrator in White Oak, Texas, uses large grocery sacks to make writing portfolios with students. The smaller version is an adaptation for this lesson.
- Making the mini paper bag portfolio:

  1. I first share with students the anatomy of a paper bag.

Flat side (no flap)

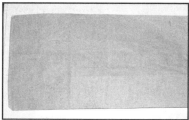

Flap side (has the folded end of the bag)

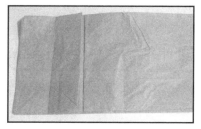

The ribs of the bag (on both sides)

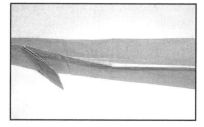

The bottom of the bag

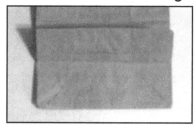

2. Students will fold the bag in half, top to bottom. This crease will be the stopping point for cutting in the next step.

3. Model for students that they will cut along the rib edge of the flat side. Both the right and left sides will be cut. Students should stop cutting when they reach the crease created when they folded the bag in half.

4. Now cutting only on the flap side, cut across the crease so that the ribs and the top half of the flap side are removed. THE FLAT SIDE SHOULD NOT BE CUT.

5. The flat side will now create the flap of the envelope (portfolio).

6. Students can shape the flap of the envelope any way they like.

7. Students should be given ten index cards to place in the bottom of their portfolio. It is important that the cards are put in the portfolio before the Velcro is affixed or the flap will not seal properly.

8. Give each student a small piece of Velcro to use to close their portfolios.

- Once the mini-portfolio is complete, go over the guideline handout with the students.
- Show them a portfolio that you have started so they have a good model.
- Students will need plenty of time to collect good samples of the word in a variety of contexts. Three to six weeks is a good time frame.
- The first entry into the portfolio is the dictionary entry. Students will neatly write a dictionary definition of their word on one of the index cards, which will be placed in the portfolio.
- After the time period for expanding the portfolio has elapsed, each student will display his or her collection of words in the class Word Gallery. Each student is given a poster board or butcher paper for this purpose. The display can be designed in class or as a homework assignment.
- Make a big deal out of the Word Gallery. Invitations can be created and sent home to parents and out to faculty members. Other classes can come explore the gallery as well.
- The day of the gallery, students explore all of the displays; classical music plays in the background, and students leave personal connection responses at five (or more) of the word displays.

- The word displays then become brilliant Word Walls (see chapter two) that continue to receive focus and instructional attention.

Evaluation/Variations:

- Many opportunities for evaluation and assessment are available for the Word Portfolios due to the extent of the activity. Grades might be given for:
  - each index card portfolio addition (minimum of ten/ 10 pts each; minimum of five/ 20 pts each)
  - word display (scored with a rubric)
  - five personal connection cards (20 pts each)
- Students, for extension, might be asked to locate examples of words from their peers' displays during their next silent sustained reading opportunity. I like to refer to this time as Silent Strategic Reading as students must be directly taught strategies for bringing meaning to texts.-.

Word Portfolio Guidelines

Like an artist, a model, a photographer or anyone that wants to illustrate to others what he or she has or has accomplished that is of value, you will create a word portfolio. This portfolio will become a valuable collection of everything you learned about your selected word.

You will collect examples of your word, in a variety of contexts for five weeks following the guidelines outlined below. During the final week of the grading period, we will be displaying our portfolios so that others can see the diversity and the variety of when, where, and how the words are used. The word portfolio collection is due:

Details about your Word Portfolio:

- Each entry will be placed on an index card.
- <u>One</u> card will be a dictionary definition of your word that includes all information about the word and its history.
- The remaining cards will be examples of instances where you see or hear the word used.
- Try to find your word in a variety of contexts: speech, music, books, cartoons, advertisements, movies, and so forth.
- When you discover an occurrence of your word, you will quote the source and include it on one of your index cards.
- You will include a minimum of 10 cards in your portfolio that illustrate your word in a variety of contexts. Each example should have occurred at different times and in different places. In other words, do not include 10 examples from the same source.
- Information on your cards should be written neatly or typed.
- Remember that portfolios are used to show the best of what someone has to offer. Spend time exploring your word and finding the various ways speakers and writers use the word.
- As always, feel free to find colorful and creative ways to design, present, and illustrate your cards and portfolio. If all of our portfolios looked exactly the same, the displays would be lifeless.

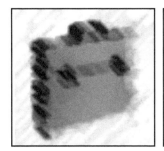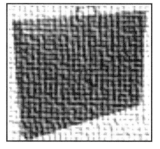

Prediction Pops

Rationale:

Based on their prior experience and knowledge of a given topic, students can predict what words may appear in a text about that topic. For example, if students are going to read a book about tornadoes, they would be able to accurately predict many of the vocabulary words that may appear in the text such as *destruction, barometric pressure, whirling, weather,* and so forth. When they exercise these prediction capabilities, students get the opportunity to rehearse and review words to which they have been previously exposed.

Predicting, a form of inference, is a critical attribute for successful reading. This strategy allows students to make predictions and then explore the outcome(s) in a multimodal, interactive way. The memory trace for the words explored is deepened and the chances of their being used and understood in new contexts are increased.

Objective:

Students will predict, based on the title and cover of a pre-selected book, seven vocabulary words that will appear in the text. Students will share why they think the words will be in the text. After the reading, students will further discuss synonyms they may have predicted, whether their words were logical for the topic, and they will then create sentences that could have appeared in the text. The discussion is crucial for this activity, as it increases awareness about word use and strengthens connections to the words discussed.

Materials:

Large packing bubbles (can be purchased at any mailing center)
Cardstock or construction paper
Markers
Labels (3/4" round)
Glue sticks
A selected text to read. Expository texts work well for this activity though any text can be used.

Presentation Guidelines:

- Depending on how many students you have and the age of those students, either make the Prediction Pops prior to the lesson or guide the students in making them. As great precision is required, the packing bubbles will need to be cut by an adult. After step one, however, students can assist in making the Prediction Pops.

Making a Prediction Pop:

1. Carefully cut a flower-shaped section (seven bubbles: one in the center and six circled around the center bubble) from the packing sheet. WARNING: One must cut carefully around the bubbles to avoid puncturing any of the air pockets. Sharp scissors are required.

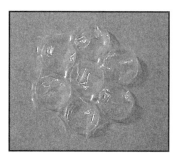

2. Using the glue sticks, glue the circular shape in the center of the cardstock or construction paper.
3. Once students have made their predictions, the seven circular labels will be gently placed on top of each bubble.

- Students will each be given a strip of seven labels. The labels come on a sheet of twenty-eight, so there are four strips of labels per sheet. It is best to cut these apart prior to the lesson to save time.
- Share with students that often before we even begin reading a book or any other text, we are able to start making predictions about the content. We can also make predictions about the vocabulary words that will appear in the text. It is important to point out that some words, like *a, and, the,* and so forth, are obvious. We are talking about larger words that may not appear in other stories about other topics.
- Choose any nonfiction text (Seymour Simon's books work well). Show the students the title and the front cover. Ask them to quietly think for a moment what words might appear in the book.
- For the purpose of example, I recently used Seymour Simon's *Wolves* to do this lesson with a group of sixth graders. To model the processes and my thinking, I said, "I really do not expect circus clowns to appear in this book. So, I will not make that prediction. Can anyone think of a word, though, that might be in this book?"
- A student suggests the word *prey.* I praise the suggestion and ask why she thinks *prey* might be in the book. In a wonderful display of prior knowledge, she explains why it would be logical for *prey* to appear in the text. Another student, who did not know or recall the term *prey,* may simply have said *food.* Through this early dialogue, many students are already learning new words or rehearsing words they could not previously recall in context.

- If other students want to borrow the words suggested by the first student, that's fine. I then ask students to predict other words that might appear in the text. Each word they think of should be written on one of the colored labels until all seven of their labels are filled in.

- After a few minutes (some students may not be able to fill all seven slots initially), ask students to share a word they predict will appear in the text. Once a suggestion is offered, be sure to ask the student why he or she thinks the word will appear in the text. Again, for the other students this provides further information about the words. As students are sharing their words, students who may not have such a strong background with the topic may borrow their peers' words. This is fine and I do not even mention it during the lesson. The reality remains that even through borrowing, they are expanding their vocabulary. Since that is the goal, it is not worth embarrassing a student who may not be able to recall seven "unique" words.

- This activity is more than vocabulary exploration; it is also a prereading strategy that brings forth prior knowledge, provides a purpose for reading, and motivates students to want to read the text to discover how accurately they predicted.

- Before reading the book, I ask students to look over their seven words again and then to turn the Prediction Pop over. I want them focusing on the text, not worrying about the words they predicted.

- Reading the book becomes quite an event. Students get excited when they hear a word that they predicted. In the reading, I try to emphasize words I know students have predicted. Students listen carefully in hopes of hearing all of the words they felt would be in the text.

Pop Fest!

- After the reading, ask students, using their thumb, to pop the bubbles of the words they accurately predicted. The sound effect of this is appealing and it helps celebrate and validate the number of accurate predictions that occurred, increasing students' confidence in their word knowledge and reading abilities.

- Discuss which words were found and why these words may have been critical to the text.

- Ask students if anyone predicted a word that was not in the text but means the same thing as a word the author used. Make sure students recall that these words are called *synonyms*. Ask students to draw a line from the word they predicted to the side of the Prediction Pop and write the synonym that appeared in the text. After a couple of students share any synonyms, ask students to pop these words as well.

- Finally, ask students if there are any of their predicted words that did not appear in the text but easily could have. Ask students to draw a line from a word that could have appeared in the text. Ask students to write a sentence, using the word that could have appeared in the text. Then allow students to pop these words as well.

- The Prediction Pops are wonderful to publish and they create another authentic Word Wall for further exploration (see chapter two).

 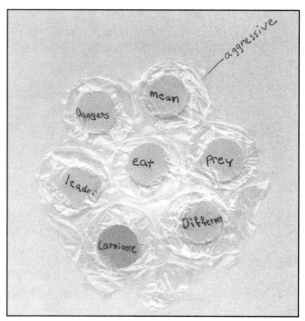

Prediction Pops made by sixth-grade student Priscilla Medrano, from Stehlik Intermediate; Houston, Texas.

Evaluation/Variations:

- Grades can be given based on the seven words predicted, synonyms, and the sentence the students add.
- Once students understand the process, you may have them only predict verbs from a given text or only predict adjectives, and so forth.

Chapter 9
Plugging In History

"It is often forgotten that (dictionaries) are artificial repositories,
put together well after the languages they define. The roots of language
are irrational and of a magical nature."

–Jorge Luis Borges, Prologue to "El otro, el mismo."

Words that we use on a daily basis are snapshots, illustrating who we are as a culture; they also tell a grand story of who we were. Like bones and artifacts exhumed from the earth by archaeologists, words give us clues about our ancient ancestors. Likewise, the thousands of words added to the 2003 version of the *Oxford English Dictionary* will one day point back in time to let future generations get a glimpse of who we are right now. These words, our language, are changed, expanded, and colored by music, art, science, technology, religion, wars, sports, and every other aspect of life that demands communication.

It is this history, these windows to the past, that sheds light on the meaning of words. By opening the windows, we provide an important layer of understanding for our students—we provide depth. Words, like people, have stories. Some stories are ancient, some are new, some are unknown, and many are in process at this moment. Sometimes new words stick and become accepted as part of the language, such as *yadda yadda yadda*, popularized on the sitcom *Seinfeld*; sometimes they flop and are never picked up by the public. When the general public uses new words, it drives their existence and gives birth to their stories. Buried in these stories are the meaning and context that energize memory.

The words and numerous synonyms in the English language are difficult enough to master; the idiomatic expressions are a nightmare for those learning English as a second language. Phrases such as "kick the bucket" must create quite a picture for those who envision someone drawing his or her leg back and giving a solid kick to a bucket. Why in the world would someone "kick the bucket"? This phrase originated on farms where the slaughter of steers for meat was an arduous task. Special hoists were devised that would pull the steer up with a rope tied to its back feet. A large bucket was often used to catch the blood, etc., from the carcass. Often the pulling of the large carcass would cause the animal's feet to loudly "kick" the large bucket. The farm expression eventually came into use to refer to any form of death.

Common modern idiomatic expressions create the same problems for those learning English. Often the expressions used by one generation baffle even English speakers of another generation. Phrases such as "kick 'em to the curb" would certainly hold little meaning for many over the age of forty and/or from some regions of the country, just as "icebox" and "five and dime" would appear odd to younger students. Again, the beauty of studying a living, dynamic language such as English lies in the cultural, generational, and geographical uses of words.

The complex richness of this language offers us great precision in our expression of ideas, feelings, and concepts. Is the water really *warm*? Or is it *lukewarm, tepid, cool, toasty, balmy,* or *sultry.* The English language, with its many synonyms, allows for an exacting specificity. By plugging in the history of our language, we plug in meaning, depth, memory, and context; we introduce our students to themselves, for they are in the process of creating the future history of our language.

Vocabulary Unplugged • ©2005 Alana Morris • www.discoverwriting.com

Birth of a Word
Developed in collaboration with Bruce Goodner

Rationale:

Every year new words are generated. These words become part of our daily speech, often without our cognitively being aware of the addition. A fun and meaningful way for students to explore and understand how words become part of our language is by examining the details of when and how these newer words become accepted into spoken and written English.

Objective:

Students will create birth announcements for recent words added to the English language. Students will explore how, when, where, and any other details that may be available for words that have been in our language less than twenty-five years. The words could be any of 6,000 new words added to the 2003 revision of the *Oxford English Dictionary*, or even newer words that are already in common use but have not yet appeared in an official form. An example of such words would be blogosphere and blogger, which are following patterns certain to land them in future editions of most dictionaries.

Materials:

Access to the Internet or printed information will be necessary
Self-created or store-bought birth announcements
See list of great websites for exploring words and their etymologies (page 144).
Markers, colors, other decorating materials

Presentation Guidelines:

- Explain to students that words have birth dates just as people do. However, words often claim whole time periods as their birth date rather than one specific day. Some words such as *sheep, ox, man*, and *woman* are incredibly old, while others like *cyberspace, telemarket*, and *instant message* are in their infancy in the life of words.
- Using the 3/5/10 brainstorming technique explained in chapter three (under Plug-in Four), generate ideas on where new words come from.
  Ideas generated may include these categories:
  Medicine
  Music
  Science
  Technology
  Education
  Sports

Literature
Movies
Television

- Have students share words they know came from each area they suggested.
- See if students can then pinpoint a year or decade when the word was first used or commonly accepted. Numerous sources can be used for this exploration: Internet, Oxford English Dictionary and/or other dictionaries, or numerous books from the library regarding the history of English words.
- A wonderful resource for finding out when older words came into use is *A History of English in Its Own Words* (1991) by Craig M. Carver. Examples of such "birth dates" include:

blooper	1937
clone	1903
Mayday	1927
thug	1839
limousine	1902
nightmare	c. 1290
love	c. 725

- Explain that within their lifetime many more words will be created and accepted into common usage.
- To celebrate the birth of some of the newest words in the English language, share that they will create a birth announcement to introduce all of the important details about a new word.
- Show students a birth announcement (these can be purchased at any stationery store, department store, or most grocery stores).
- Encourage students to be creative with what they put down for some of the details such as weight, height, parents, and so forth. Students can also add details to the announcement that may be important for their word.
- Students can brainstorm possible words, research the words, and create the birth announcement alone or with a partner.
- Birth announcements should be creatively published once they have been shared.

Information typically included on birth announcements:
Name, date, time, weight, height, parents, and occasionally siblings

Evaluation:

A rubric should be created to assess this assignment. One of the objectives for this lesson is the light research involved. This will be an important component of the assessment.

See sample of birth announcement for "mouse potato."

Announcing the Arrival
of the Latest Member of the
LEXICON Family!

MOUSE POTATO

was born in 1993.

Proud Single parent:	*Writer Alice Kahn*
Weight:	*Heavy in the technology area*
Sibling:	*Couch Potato*
Characteristics:	*Noun; used to describe someone who spends a lot of time at the computer.*

Word Warp Time Line

Rationale:

An important historical exploration of words involves how one area, discipline, or concept changes over time. This type of word study provides students with an opportunity to see how time, other cultures, and change impact words.

Objective:

Students will choose one field of study, word, or concept and explore how it has changed over time. Students will create a time line that shows important dates related to their word(s).

Example: The word *woman* has changed throughout time and continues to change. Historically, there are numerous reasons for this, but it is interesting to note when changes occurred.

A time line is an ideal graphic for illustrating the changes to a word or idea.

Woman comes from the Old English compound word *wifman: wif* = wife and *man* = human being. Then when the Norsemen (Vikings) invaded England, *female* came into the English language. *Chick* first appeared in 1927 but became popular in the 1960's, and hip-hop and rap music have brought *shorty* on board. *Gal, girl,* and *missy* could be added onto the time line as well.

Materials:

Access to the Internet for research and/or language history books. There are several books and websites available that give detailed information about the history of words. Paper, markers, and other needed supplies for publishing the time line.
Register tape or sentence strips are good to use for time lines.

Presentation Guidelines:

- The Word Warp Time Line is intended to be an exploration of terms and not a scientific document. Any term related to the word, discipline, or concept is fine. The idea is for students to see how words change over time.
- Brainstorm, with students, words or entire fields (such as technology) where words have slowly (or quickly) been added or where words have changed.

  Possible suggestions include:
  Music, Medicine, Education, Technology, Coffee, Skateboarding, Basketball
  **Basically this list will be similar to the list generated by asking where new words come from in Plug-in Twenty-eight.

- Then students should, alone or with a partner, research their selected area.
- Students will create a time line of the important word(s) or concepts, indicating the time period or approximate dates when the word(s) became important and a brief explanation with each date (time period).
- Students should be encouraged to select words or topics that generate at least four dates for the time line.
- The final time line should be colorful and informative.

Evaluation/Variations:

- Word Warp Time Lines can be created using topics from other content areas that are current topics of study.
- A rubric should be used to score the final time line. You may decide to give separate grades for the research and planning involved.

Word Passports

Rationale:

Another concept related to history that provides depth of understanding for students is the exploration of words in the English language that come from other countries. Many of our words are not only from other time periods but from other cultures as well. Examining these words raises students' awareness of how words come into a language and provides a context for remembering them. This is a wonderful opportunity to connect geography, world cultures, and history to word study.

Objective:

Students will create a passport for words that have come into English from another country. All known details about the word will be included in the passport. The passports will then be published to show how frequently words are borrowed (and never returned!) from other cultures. Maps should, in some way, be included in the publication process.

Materials:

Maps
Passport (if possible)
Access to the Internet or other etymology resources
Removable labels (return address size works well)
Paper
Stapler
Cardstock (for passport cover)

Presentation Guidelines:

- Using a large world map, ask students if they know of any words in the English language that come from other countries. If they do, ask them to come up to the map and point to the location the word came from. Most students, at this point, will be limited in what they will be able to share.

- Read *The Journey of English* by Donna Brook or information culled from various sources about the early days of the English language. The idea is for students to understand that a serious of invasions over time changed and shaped our language. In today's information age, the invasions are not warlike, but words still "invade" our language from a variety of sources. Many countries take words from the English language as well. Some countries would prefer that these English words stay on our side of the ocean so their language remains "pure." However, there are no boundaries or immigration procedures for words.

- If you have a passport or can obtain one, it is nice to show students a real passport. However, it is not essential.

- Share with students that people must have a passport when traveling to another country. The passport includes: their country of origin, full legal name, date of birth, passport number, place of birth, and then pages so that the owner of the passport can obtain immigration stamps in each country visited (this is not done so much now; stamps often have to be requested).

- The cover of the passport typically has the country seal and the name of the country. It also has PASSPORT printed clearly at the top. The colors vary from country to country.

- Students will search for a word that comes from another country and will create a passport for that word that includes the information, as accurately as possible, that would be found in a person's passport. There is room for creativity. Exact date of birth may not be available. Approximate dates or full time period can be used instead.

- Once students know their word and its country of origin, have them write the word on one of the removable labels and place it on the map. At this point, no other student should choose this word. It is neat to see the words slowly appear on the map. Students can note and discuss patterns regarding words that have come into the English language.

- At the close of the activity, allow time for a few students to share their passports. It is often a good idea to share only a few words a day. Otherwise, students lose their listening focus and the whole purpose of sharing is lost.

Evaluation/Variations:

- Throughout the year, as students locate other words that have come from other countries, they can request a label to add each word to the map.

- Once again, a rubric provides the best method for scoring the Word Passports so that the objectives that are taught and expected are what is assessed and scored.

Sampling of Wonderful Word Websites

*Warning: These sites are addictive and may consume hours of word lovers' time!

www.behindthename.com/ History of first names

www.dictionary.com Great online dictionary, which is the host for a *Word of the Day* option.

www.doubletongued.org/ Incredible site for exploring more words than you have time to explore!

www.etymonline.com Great online etymology dictionary

www.freevocabulary.com/ 5,000 collegiate words and brief definitions for preparing for standardized tests.

www.fun-with-words.com/ This site offers multiple ways to explore words and word play.

www.funwords.com/ Great site for exploring the fun of delight of the English language.

www.highspeedplus.com/~edonon/linguist.htm Linguistic archaeology

www.kokogiak.com/logolepsy/ Collection and exploration of obscure English words

www.krysstal.com/english.html Another great site for exploring the origins and history of the English language

www.phrases.org.uk History of English phrases and sayings

www.word-detective.com/ Newspaper column that answers question about words. Awesome site!

www.wordfocus.com/ Focuses on Latin and Greek elements of the English language

www.wordorigins.org History of word origins. Great site!

www.wordorigins.org/histeng.htm Brief history of the English language

www.wordphiles.info/image-word-unit1/image-word-set1.html Illustrated List of words

www.wordspy.com Great for exploring the latest additions to our vocabulary.

www.worldwidewords.org/index.htm History of words across the world.

Bibliography

Introduction

Pinker, Steven. 1994. *The Language Instinct.* New York: Harper Perennial.

Prologue: Plugging in Guidance

Pearson, P. David, and M. C. Gallagher. 1983. "The Instruction of Reading Comprehension." *Contemporary Educational Psychology* 8:317–44.

Chapter 1: Plugging in Memory

Baddeley, Alan. 1998. *Human Memory: Theory and Practice.* Boston: Allyn and Bacon.

———. 1999. *Essentials of Human Memory.* London: Psychology Press.

Baddeley, Alan, Martin Conway, and John Aggleton, eds. 2001. *Episodic Memory: New Directions in Research.* New York: Oxford University Press.

Buzan, Tony. 1993. *The Mind Map Book.* New York: Dutton Books.

Carroll, Joyce Armstrong, and Ron Habermas. 1996. *Jesus Didn't Use Worksheets: A 2000 Year Old Model for Good Teaching.* Spring, Tex.: Absey and Co.

Carroll, Joyce Armstrong, and Eddie Wilson, comps. 1997. *Poetry After Lunch: Poems to Read Aloud.* Spring, Tex.: Absey & Co.

Clements, Andrew. 2001. *Double Trouble in Walla Walla.* New York: Digital Books.

Ebbinghaus, H. (1885). *Über das Gedchtnis. Untersuchungen zur experimentellen Psychologie.* Leipzig: Duncker & Humblot; the English edition is Ebbinghaus, H. (1913). *Memory. A Contribution to Experimental Psychology.* New York: Teachers College, Columbia University (Reprinted Bristol: Thoemmes Press, 1999).

Gardner, Howard. 1983. *Frames of Mind: The Theory of Multiple Intelligences.* New York: Basic Books.

Gathercole, Susan E., and Alan Baddeley. 1993. *Working Memory and Language.* Hove: Lawrence Erlbaum Associates, Publishers.

Jensen, Eric. 1995. *Brain-Based Learning and Teaching.* Del Mar, Calif.: Turning Point Publishing.

———. 1998. *Teaching with the Brain in Mind.* Alexandria, Virginia: Association of Supervision and Curriculum Development.

Langer, Ellen. 1997. *The Power of Mindful Learning.* Reading, Mass.: Merloyd Lawrence Books.

Restak, Richard. 2003. *The New Brain: How the Modern Age Is Rewiring Your Mind.* Emmaus, Pennsylvania: Rodale.

Schacter, Daniel, ed. 1995. *Memory Distortion: How the Minds, Brains, and Societies Reconstruct the Past.* Cambridge, Mass.: Harvard University Press.

————. 1996. *Searching for Memory: The Brain, the Mind, and the Past*. New York: Basic Books.

————. 2001. *Seven Sins of Memory: How the Mind Forgets and Remembers*. Boston: Houghton Mifflin.

Chapter 2: Plugging in Wordplay

Caine, Renate, and Geoffrey Caine. 1994. *Making Connections: Teaching and the Human Brain*. Alexandria, Virginia: Association for Supervision and Curriculum Development (ASCD).

Cleary, Brain. 1996. *It Looks a Lot Like Reindeer*. New York: Lerner.

————. 1996. *Give Me Back My Schubert*. New York: Lerner.

Demasio, Antonio. 1994. *Descartes' Error: Emotion, Reason, and the Human Brain*. New York: G. P. Putnam's Sons.

Farb, Peter. 1973. *Word Play*. New York: Vintage Books.

Hobson, J. Allan. 1994. *The Chemistry of Conscious States*. Boston: Little, Brown.

Jensen, Eric. 1996. *The Learning Brain*. Del Mar, Calif.: Turning Point Publishing.

————. 1998. *Teaching with the Brain in Mind*. Alexandria, Virginia: Association for Supervision and Curriculum Development.

Kline, Peter. 1988. *The Everyday Genius*. Arlington, Virginia: Great Ocean Publishers.

Langer, Ellen. 1989. *Mindfulness*. Reading, Mass.: Addison-Wesley Publishing.

Lecourt, Nancy. 1992. *Abracadabra to ZigZag*. New York: Puffin Books.

Lederer, Richard. 1988. *Get Thee to a Punnery*. Charleston, S.C.: Wyrick and Company.

Lederer, Richard. 1996. *Pun and Games*. Chicago, Illinois: Chicago Review Press.

Nachmanovitch, Stephen. 1990. *Free Play: The Power of Improvisation in Life and the Arts*. New York: G. P. Putnam's Sons.

Seligman, Martin E. P. 1990. *Learned Optimism: How to Change Your Mind and Your Life*. New York: Pocket Books.

Von Oech, Roger. 1990. *A Whack on the Side of the Head: How You Can Be More Creative*. Stamford, Conn.: U.S. Games Systems.

Walton, Rick. 1998. *Why the Banana Split*. Layton, Utah: Gibbs Smith Publisher.

Webster's Synonyms, Antonyms, and Homonyms. 1994 Edition. New York: Crescent Books.

Chapter 3: Plugging in Movement

Fry, Edward Bernard. 1993. *The Reading Teacher's Books of Lists, Third Edition*. New York: Prentice Hall.

Gardner, Howard. 1983. *Frames of Mind: The Theory of Multiple Intelligences*. New York: Basic Books.

Hannaford, Carla. *Smart Moves: Why Learning Is Not All in Your Head*. Arlington, Virginia: Great Ocean Publishers.

Hobson, J. Allan. 1994. *The Chemistry of Conscious States*. Boston: Little, Brown.

Houston, Jean. 1982. *The Possible Human*. New York: G. P. Putnam's Sons.

John-Steiner, Vera. 1995. *Notebooks of the Mind*. New York: Oxford University Press.

Chapter 4: Plugging in Patterns

Caine, Renate, and Geoffrey Caine. 1994. *Making Connections: Teaching and the Human Brain*. Alexandria, Virginia: Association for Supervision and Curriculum Development.

———. 1997. *Education on the Edge of Possibility*. Alexandria, Virginia: Association for Supervision and Curriculum Development.

Cunningham, Patricia. 1995. *Phonics They Use: Words for Reading and Writing*. New York: Harper Collins.

Hart, Leslie. 1983. *Human Brain and Human Learning*. Covington, Washington: Books for Educators, Inc.

Jackendoff, Ray. 1994. *Patterns in the Mind*. New York: Basic Books.

Laminack, Lester L., and Katie Wood. 1996. *Spelling in Use*. Urbana, Illinois: National Council of Teachers of English.

Langer, Ellen. 1997. *The Power of Mindful Learning*. Reading, Mass.: Addison-Wesley.

Sylwester, Robert. 1995. *Celebration of Neurons*. Alexandria, Virginia: Association for Supervision and Curriculum Development.

Volk, Tyler. 1995. *Metapatterns*. New York: Columbia University Press.

Chapter 5: Plugging in Color

Birren, Faber. 1978. *Color and Human Response*. New York: Van Nostrand Reinhold.

Howard, Pierce J. 1994. *The Owner's Manual for the Brain: Everyday Applications from Mind-Brain Research*. Austin, Tex.: Leornian Press.

Huyghe, Rene. 1977. "Color and Interior Time." *Color Symbolism*. Ed. Adolph Portmann. Dallas: Spring Publications, Inc.

Jensen, Eric. 1995. *Brain-Based Learning and Teaching*. Del Mar, Calif.: Turning Point Publishing.

John-Steiner, Vera. 1997. *Notebooks of the Mind*. New York: Oxford University Press.

Kenyon, Tom. 1994. *Brain States*. Naples, Fla.: United States Publishing.

Luscher, Max. 1969. *Color Test*. Trans. Ian Scott. New York: Washington Square Press.

Nordine, Ken. 2000. *Colors*. San Diego, California: Harcourt Brace Jovanovich.

Rossotti, Hazel. 1983. *Colour: Why the World Isn't Grey*. Princeton, N.J.: Princeton University Press.

Walker, Morton. 1991. *The Power of Color*. Garden City Park, N.Y.: Avery Publishing Group, Inc.

Chapter 6: Plugging in Music and Sound

Cunningham, Patricia. 1995. *Phonics They Use: Words for Reading and Writing*. New York: Harper Collins.

Jackendoff, Ray. 1994. *Patterns in the Mind: Language and Human Nature*. New York: Basic Books.

Jourdain, Robert. 1997. *Music, the Brain, and Ecstasy: How Music Captures Our Imagination*. New York: William Morrow and Company.

Kenyon, Tom. 1994. *Brain States*. Naples, Fla.: United States Publishing.

Kohut, Daniel L. 1985. *Musical Performance: Learning Theory and Pedagogy*. Englewood Cliffs, N.J.: Prentice Hall.

Kotulak, Ronald. 1996. *Inside the Brain: Revolutionary Discoveries of How the Mind Works*. Kansas City, Mo.: Andrews and McMeel Books.

MacNeil, Robert. 1989. *WordStruck*. New York: Viking Penguin.

Miller, George. 1996. *The Science of Words*. New York: Scientific American Library.

Rothstein, Edward. 1995. *Emblems of the Mind: The Inner Life of Music and Mathematics*. New York: Avon Books.

Russell, Peter. 1979. *The Brain Book*. New York: Plume Books.

Storr, Anthony. 1992. *Music and the Mind*. New York: Ballantine Books.

Swanwick, Keith. 1988. *Music, Mind, and Education*. London: Routledge.

Chapter 7: Plugging in Poetry

Algarín, Miguel, and Bob Holman, eds. 1994. *Aloud: Voices from the Nuyorican Poets Café*. New York: Henry Holt and Company.

Behn, Robin, and Chase Twichell, eds. 1992. *The Practice of Poetry: Writing Exercises from Poets Who Teach*. New York: Harper Perennial.

Dillard, Annie. 1995. *Mornings Like This: Found Poems*. New York: Harper Perennial.

Janeczko, Paul, comp. 2002. *Seeing the Blue Between: Advice and Inspiration for Young Poets*. Cambridge, Mass.: Candlewick Press.

Livingston, Myra Cohn. 1990. *Climb the Bell Tower: Essays on Poetry*. New York: Harper and Row.

McVeigh-Schultz, Jane and Mary Lynn Ellis. 1997. *With a Poet's Eye: Children Translate the World*. Portsmouth, New Hampshire: Heinemann.

Muller, Lauren, ed. 1995. *June Jordan's Poetry for the People: A Revolutionary Blueprint*. New York: Routledge.

Oliver, Mary. 1994. *A Poetry Handbook*. San Diego: Harcourt Brace and Company.

Perrine, Laurence, and Thomas R. Arp. 1992. *Sound and Sense: An Introduction to Poetry, Eighth Edition*. Fort Worth: Harcourt Brace Jovanovich College Publishers.

Smith, Frank. 1997. *Reading Without Nonsense: Third Edition*. New York: Teachers College Press.

Chapter 8: Plugging in Context

Cunningham, A. E., and K. E. Stanovitch. 1991. "Tracking the Unique Effects of Print Exposure in Children: Associations with Vocabulary, General Knowledge and Spelling." *Journal of Educational Psychology* 83:264–74.

Gathercole, Susan E., and Alan Baddeley. 1993. *Working Memory and Language*. Hove, United Kingdom: Lawrence Erlbaum Associates, Publishers.

Langer, Ellen. 1997. *The Power of Mindful Learning*. Reading, Mass.: Merloyd Lawrence Books.

Pinker, Steven. 1994. *The Language Instinct*. New York: Harper Perennial.

Schneider, Meg F. 1997. *Word Power: Essential Tools for Building a Solid Vocabulary*. New York: Simon and Schuster.

Chapter 9: Plugging in History

Baugh, Albert C., and Thomas Cable. 1993. *A History of the English Language, Fourth Edition*. Englewood Cliffs, N.J.: Prentice Hall.

Brook, Donna. 1998. *The Journey of English*. New York: Clarion Books.

Bryson, Bill. 1990. *Mother Tongue: English and How It Got That Way*. New York: Avon Books.

Carver, Craig M. 1991. *A History of English in Its Own Words*. New York: Barnes and Noble Books.

Garrison, Webb. 1992. *Why You Say It: The Fascinating Stories Behind Over 600 Everyday Words and Phrases*. New York: MJF Books.

McCrum, Robert, et al. 1992. *The Story of English*. New York: Penguin Books.

Muschell, David. 1990. *Where in the Word? Extraordinary Stories Behind 801 Ordinary Words*. Rocklin, Calif.: Prima Publishing.

Winchester, Simon. 1998. *The Professor and the Madman: A Tale of Murder, Insanity, and the Making of the Oxford English Dictionary*. New York: Harper Perennial.